BATTLE OF THE
TWO TALMUDS

BATTLE OF THE TWO TALMUDS

Judaism's Struggle with Power, Glory, & Guilt

LEON H. CHARNEY

AND

SAUL MAYZLISH

Edited by Renée Paley-Bain

BARRICADE BOOKS

FORT LEE, NEW JERSEY

Published by Barricade Books Inc.
185 Bridge Plaza North
Suite 309
Fort Lee, NJ 07024

www.barricadebooks.com

Library of Congress Cataloging-in-Publication Data

Charney, Leon H.
  Battle of the two Talmuds : Judaism's struggle with power, glory, and guilt / by Leon H.
Charney and Saul Mayzlish ; edited by Renee Paley-Bain.
    p. cm.
  ISBN 978-1-56980-439-1
  1. Judaism--History--Talmudic period, 10-425. 2. Jews--Identity. 3. Talmud--Criticism,
Redaction. 4. Talmud Yerushalmi--Criticism, Redaction. 5. Jews--Iraq--Babylonia--
History. I. Maizlish, Sha'ul. II. Title.
  BM177.C43 2010
  296.09'015--dc22
                2009050681

ISBN 13: 978-1-56980-439-1
ISBN 1-56980-439-7

10 9 8 7 6 5 4 3 2 1

Manufactured in the United States of America

CONTENTS

DEDICATIONS

*Dedicated to my children, Mickey and Nati, to help them under-
stand that study and the advancement of knowledge are essential
for a better world.*

LHC

*Dedicated to the memory of my beloved cousin Meidi (Malka)
Mehler.*

SM

"...the Talmud is perhaps the only sacred book in all of the world culture that permits and even encourages the student to question it."

—Adin Steinsaltz, *The Essential Talmud*

Acknowledgments

To Renée Paley-Bain, for whose wonderful editing and stringent commitment to perfection we owe tremendous gratitude. Most likely, this book could not have seen the light of day without her contribution.

To Carole Stuart, my publisher, who has shown a great understanding of a potential of books that examine all aspects of Jewish history.

To Professor Natti Laor for his strong guidance, illumination, and dedication that contributed enormously to the efficacy of this book. He is a renowned psychiatrist, philosopher, and Talmudic scholar, and his keen observations have been extremely important and integral to the understanding of some of the complexities in the text.

To Dr. Charles Friedlander, a renowned physician with a tremendous knowledge of Jewish history, who has been inspirational to me in my writing books on Jewish subjects.

To my office staff, Bruce Block, Rob Essex, Nikki Istrefovic and Marissa Dockery, who have been extraordinarily patient and understanding of my time commitment and have always encouraged my writing.

To Edna Lavie for her help in excellently translating the Hebrew manuscripts.

To the Bar-Ilan University Library staff for their erudition and guidance.

To the librarians of the Rambam Library in Beyt Ariela, Tel Aviv.

To the following researchers who were enormously helpful: Rabbi Dr. Yitzchak Alfasi, the Hasidut researcher; Akiva Zimmerman, researcher of the prayer and cantorial (*hazanut*) field; and Rabbi Avraham Hacohen Blas, researcher of the treasure of the Jerusalem Talmud, for their valuable assistance.

PREFACE

$\mathcal{W}$E WERE SITTING in Café Alternative, a popular Tel Aviv café where many families who eat only kosher food go for an evening out. Saul Mayzlish and I had spent many nights here working on our book, *The Mystery of the Kaddish*, which was published first in the United States (2006) and later in Israel. I thought of this café as a suitable anthropological habitat for reviewing the many responses we received in regard to that book, which traced the history of the prayer recited by mourners after the death of a close relative. Saul was convinced that the reason behind its success was the same as the one underlying the adoption of the *Kaddish* by the Jewish people at the time of the Crusades and later during the plague known as the Black Death: In those grim days, as today, Jews felt alienated and isolated. Now, as then, they are looking for support, courage, and a divine and national link.

The conversation turned to U.S.–Israel relations and the attitude of American-born Jews, of whom I am one. "The *Kaddish*," I said, "is more popular today in America than the *Shema*.[1] People who don't identify themselves as Jews—do not belong to a congregation or synagogue, and do not send their children to a Jewish school—don't even have the opportunity to learn about the *Shema*. Yet they will go to their grandfather's or father's funeral, and maybe even sit *shiva*, keep the *yahrzeit*.[2] So, as a matter of course, they'll be exposed to the *Kaddish*."

We laughed. *Kaddish*, it seems, is the mark that distinguishes you as a person who deliberates about your Jewish identity versus your American nationality, a person who reflects upon this rift between Americanness and Jewishness or even pro-Israeli Jewishness.

Saul said, "This dichotomy is a modern version of a more ancient episode in our history: the Babylonian Exile. Even then, during the first exile, in the aftermath of the

---

[1] The most important prayer in Judaism, recited twice a day. It begins "Hear, O Israel: the Lord is our God, the Lord is One." The *Shema* is considered the Jewish "confession of faith" and is a vital part of the liturgy. It is recited by a Jew on his or her deathbed. Throughout the centuries, Jews undergoing martyrdom have died with the *Shema* on their lips.

[2] To "sit *shiva*" is to observe the seven-day mourning period following a funeral, when friends and relatives visit the bereaved family. Many of the ancient observances are still maintained, but in a modernized version. For instance, the family now sits on low stools during the mourning period, rather than on overturned couches and beds, as was typical in earlier days. A candle burns continuously for the seven days. The *yahrzeit* is the Hebrew calendar's anniversary of the death, which is commemorated by close family; a memorial candle is lit and the *Kaddish* or mourner's prayer is recited.

destruction of the First Temple, and again after the Second Temple was destroyed, the Jewish people were torn between their loyalty to the land of their forefathers, the Land of Israel, and their new home in Babylonia, where they or their ancestors had fled. They had to adapt themselves to life in the new land and to the new condition of living together with non-Jews, leaving their brethren behind in the Land of Israel. This is also the background for the creation of the two Talmuds: the Jerusalem and the Babylonian."[3]

"This comparison is very interesting," I mused. "We often speak about New York, my city, as the new Babylon, a city where, from a Jewish point of view, it is possible to lead a full Jewish life. But there are other elements, historical and psychological. Could it be that along with their desire to remain in Babylonia, within that Jewish autonomy—which boasted a president, an exilarch (prince of the exiles),[4] and sages—they also developed the well-known Jewish guilt complex toward their brethren who remained in the Land of Israel, poor in both spirit and material wealth?"

"Well," Saul said, "In order to have a clear conscience, the Babylonians would send a local sage from time to time to see how the Jews were faring in the inferior land."

"There may be a measure of hypocrisy in this," I replied, "something insincere. I read that they even made a ruling that it was forbidden to leave Babylonia, but not the Land of Israel."

Saul suggested that we focus on questions that stem from this conflict: Was the foundation of the Jerusalem Talmud

---

[3] The Talmuds are two great records of academic discussion and of judicial administration of Jewish law (*halakhah*) compiled over centuries by scholars and jurists in several countries. They both codify and interpret the commandments in the Torah.

[4] The exilarch was the title of the head of the Babylonian Jewry, one of the leaders of the exiled community, a prince descended from the royal house of King David.

co-opted by the Babylonian Talmud and did the Babylonian Talmud take over Judaism? Could the Babylonian Talmud be responsible for a significant modification and/or transformation of Judaism?

I added some questions of my own. The Torah commands Jews to live in the Holy Land. How did the Babylonian Talmudists rationalize their appropriation of the foundation of Judaism? Is there a connection between Jewish guilt then and now over such acts of expropriation?

"No less fascinating," said Saul, "is the question of continuity, the lines of development linking the Babylonia/Israel conflict with the future of the Jewish people as they wander throughout Europe. The influence of the sages of the Land of Israel spread in the direction of Ashkenaz (Germany and France), whereas Spanish and North African Jewry came under the influence of Babylonia. How did all this take shape, after hundreds of years, and filter down to the modern Babylon, in America? And how does the existence of Israel affect the modern Jew and the biblical injunction to live in the Holy Land?"

"Saul, I think this is worth a journey, no less than the one we took in search of the *Kaddish*. Let's get started."

Leon H. Charney
New York, New York

Introduction

*I*n this book, we hope to examine one of the most crucial episodes in the chronicles of the Jewish people: the establishment of two works of critical importance to Jewish life, culture, and observance: the Jerusalem Talmud and the Babylonian Talmud. We'll look at how the one that developed outside the Holy Land— the one created in the Diaspora—came to be the predominant influence on the Jewish people throughout the world. And we'll consider the trail of consequences that that predominant influence brought about, including its lasting impression on Jewish life today. There is no objective history of the Babylonian era of Judaism, a period of approximately 750 years. Everything we know about it comes from the Babylonian Talmud itself, which could be considered self-serving. We have a duty to study this era and put together a record of what transpired in that period.

In the history of the Jews, when oppression by a series of conquering empires led to privation and suffering among the people of Israel, large masses fled the Holy Land to take up life elsewhere. This was the Diaspora, the dispersion of Jews to other countries. Many found sanctuary in Babylonia, where a Jewish community was established that not only flourished economically but also became a seat of higher learning with biblical scholars on a level with, and competing with, those who remained behind in the Holy Land. The sages in Babylonia, with the freedom to devote to their studies and the ambition to prove their scholarship equal or superior to that of the scholars in the Holy Land, produced one of the greatest works of Jewish writing: the Babylonian Talmud.

The Babylonian Talmud, however, was not the first. It was based upon the Jerusalem Talmud, which had been initiated 150 years earlier and was still being developed when work began on the Babylonian version. And yet the Babylonian Talmud became the principal source of Jewish study and Jewish law, superseding the Jerusalem Talmud. The Jerusalem scholars became subordinate to their brethren in Babylonia.

How did this come about? How did the Jews of Babylonia, along with their leaders and scholars, overtake those of the Land of Israel? Could it be because of the inexorable principle: "The rich man gains the upper hand" (*Mishnah Bava Metzia* 87:2)? Babylonian Jewry did indeed enjoy material success—in contrast to the poverty and repression in the Land of Israel—as well as the power derived from it. Today, too, the power of wealth can lead to cultural and spiritual authority.

For many years Babylonian scholars had "made *aliyah*," returning to Israel to consult with the sages there and study at their academies. *Aliyah,* or return to the Holy Land, comes from the Hebrew word for "ascent." Israel was still considered the center of Jewish spirituality, so those returning were "ascending" to the Holy Land. In fact, Babylonian Talmudists could not receive ordination in Babylonia; they had to come to Israel to be ordained. Yet when the Jewish settlement in the Land of Israel was deteriorating—sources of livelihood had dried up, edicts and taxes had become unbearable burdens—*aliyah* from the Diaspora to the Holy Land stopped altogether.

The decline of the Land of Israel was indeed physical, but why did this jeopardize its spiritual centrality?

There are 613 commandments in the Torah, one of them the commandment that a Jew must live in Israel. The Land of Israel was the holy place for all of the Jewish people. So it seems that we have a contradiction. The brilliant rabbis who formulated the Babylonian Talmud certainly knew of this commandment but chose to stay in Babylonia and forsook their Talmudic brethren who stayed in Israel and completed the Jerusalem Talmud. The Jerusalem rabbis were much poorer than those in Babylonia and had greater restrictions on their ability to create their Talmud.

The sages of Babylonia supported the idea that substitution was possible; one did not have to live in the Holy Land to satisfy the commandment of the Torah. Thus during the course of a remarkable era, the Babylonian center empowered itself, and it grew and prospered. In Babylonia it became convenient to put aside the memory of the terrible catastrophe that had befallen the Jewish nation and its land. Babylonia became the bastion of Torah scholarship, the study of sacred texts of Judaism, during a time that boasted of not only economic growth but also political stability. It was the antithesis of the Land of Israel; depleted, oppressed, and self-doubting, Israel could not compete with Babylonia, either in scholarship or in wisdom. It was relegated to a secondary position, disgraced from within and without, while Babylonia was crowned as the thriving spiritual center.

The sages in the Holy Land, such as Rabbi Ami, had no qualms about expressing their indignation with their counterparts in Babylonia: "How they adorn themselves there in Babylonia, the sons of the Torah, in pleasant garments and luxurious raiment? It appears that they are not sons of the Torah."

On the other hand, Rabbi Yochanan was displeased with the critical remark. He defended the Babylonian Talmudists, describing them as *talmidei hahamim* (Torah scholars) in every sense of the word: "But all their trappings and adornments are meant to assuage the distress of being in exile and the alienation they feel in the foreign land."

This sentiment also appears to underlie the statement by Rabbi Yoseph of Babylonia. He claims that the verse "[In days] to come Jacob shall strike root; they will bud and show blossom—Israel" (Isaiah 27:6) is actually referring to the sages of Babylonia, who are portrayed in the Talmud as "Making blossoms and flowers for the Torah" (*Shabbat* 145b). So, according to Rabbi Yoseph, "Jacob shall strike root" in Babylonia, Israel shall blossom and flower in Babylonia, and the land, Babylonia, shall be filled with wisdom. This statement may also be an underlying allusion to the pain and sorrow associated with the longing for the messianic era and the continued exile.

Nonetheless, we are still left with the profoundly disturbing question: Why did this sojourn in Babylonia become so comfortable, the people so pretentious and haughty, practical and self-seeking, finally reconciling themselves to remaining in exile and in so doing realizing the brilliance and glory they achieved?

Our research indicates that there was tremendous guilt by the Babylonian Talmudists over the fact that they had abandoned the Land of Israel and established this huge vibrant Jewish community in Babylonia. One could say the guilt is manifested in many ways, such as sending messengers from Babylonia to Jerusalem to assist the Jerusalem Talmudists monetarily. In addition, our research found that the Babylonian Talmudists felt so guilty about their position that they created a theory that Abraham's birthplace of Mesopotamia was the true Holy Land of the Jewish people. Thus they made arguments to the effect that Mesopotamia was part of God's commandment to live in the Holy Land. (Perhaps we could make an argument that Saddam Hussein was a descendant of the Jewish people under such rationalization.)

Of course, it is impossible to discredit an entire Diaspora group, certainly not one that did such an extraordinary job of constructing abiding Torah scholarship. And, in the words of the time-honored adage, "no transgression extinguishes Torah scholarship." Nevertheless, we cannot ignore statements like "the tribe of arrogant founders that gathered in their yeshiva." The sages in Babylonia must have infuriated Rabbi Ami to such an extent that—as the head of the Yeshiva in Tiberias in 279–280 CE—he used invectives, which had never before appeared in the Talmudic lexicon, in his condemnation of those who benefited by leaving Israel: "He who eats of Babylonia's soil, it is as if he eats the flesh of his ancestors" (*Shabbat* 113b). An expansion of this diatribe is found in a commentary in the *Kedoshim* tractate or treatise: "Some say it is like eating insects and bugs" (*Zebachim* 113b).

In a biting ironic tone, his colleague Rabbi Shimon ben Elazar denigrates Babylonian wealth and haughtiness by echoing earlier statements in the Torah: "Jews outside of the Land of Israel [are like] idolaters...." And only when real danger arises—the existential life-and-death danger about the future of the Land of Israel (the diminishing number of Jews, weakening of Torah study, the lowering of morale and local unity)—do important intellectual personalities such as Rabbi Abba bar Kahana, a student of his masters Rabbi Yochanan, Resh Lakish, and Rabbi Elazar, voice their concern and propose a way to alter the relationship, expressing the opinion that if he should see full vessels of Babylonia in the Land of Israel, he would know the Messiah was coming. In other words, *aliyah* from the Babylonian exile to the Land of Israel had the potential to rescue the Holy Land from oblivion.

In any event, it is clear that there was tension and strong resentment. Nonetheless, the idea of waves of *aliyah* was a pipedream. In reality, the dominant trend was in the opposite direction: massive emigration of students from the Land of Israel to Babylonia, reinforcing and strengthening the learning centers there. Their material and social wellbeing, along with pride in their Torah scholarship, increased to such an extent that Babylonia became, in their eyes, equal in status to the Land of Israel: "anyone who lives in Babylonia it is as if he lives in the Land of Israel" (*Ketubot* 111a). And those who emigrated were called "our masters who emigrated from the Land of Israel" (Rav Hasda, *Ta 'anit* 23b).

The temptation to emigrate was enormous. Babylonia promised sources of livelihood, economic prosperity (there were no charity funds in Babylonia), and above all, a full Jewish life— the opposite of the poverty and emptiness that characterized the spiritual realm of the Land of Israel. Fewer and fewer took the opposite route, *aliyah*, which dwindled to such an extent that the Christians became the majority in the Land of Israel, albeit a small one. And from the spiritual point of view, the Torah centers became drastically reduced in size. The Land of the Forefathers remained wanting, an empty shell, down to the lowest level of poverty.

The separation of Babylonia from the Land of Israel was so devastating that the sages feared that the capacity for Talmudic study and creativity would be lost in the Land of our Forefathers, which was no longer producing Torah scholars (the outcome of edicts, socioeconomic conditions, shrinking population). There was concern about the community's very survival and the thought that it might, heaven forbid, even disappear. The suspension of learning caused the evaporation of an enormous reservoir of Jewish knowledge. The chronicles of the Jewish people have shown us that Judaism without Talmud scholarship is destined to perish. Without a healthy, vital tradition of learning, even Torah scholars cannot continue to build up and develop a community of scholarship. Such a situation leads to the adoption of alien values, assimilation, and eventually the dissolution of historic and communal continuity. Without continuous renewal, Jewish knowledge that involves interaction among all the members of the community will cease, respect for the divine will also be undermined, and Jewish creativity will be silenced.

The danger to the continued development of the center in the Land of Israel was already apparent when the process began of redacting the Mishnah, writing down what had until then been an oral tradition. With the death of the redactor Rabbi Judah Ha-Nasi, the strength of the Land of Israel in the realm of Torah scholarship began to wane alongside political and economic decline. It was then that the emigration began. Even great rabbinical scholars who had immigrated to the Land of Israel from Babylonia, such as Abba Arikha—who had accompanied his uncle Rabbi Hiyya, a student and colleague of Rabbi Judah Ha-Nasi and a member of the courts (*Sanhedrin*)—had a change of mind. In the end, he decided to settle in Sura, Babylonia, where he built a dynamic world of Talmud scholarship. (See Chapter 2.)

This book is not meant to cast aspersions on the Babylonian Talmud, but its aim is to foster a better understanding since not much is written about the paradoxical differences between the two Talmuds and about their origination. It obviously goes to the heart of what is meant by Judaism. Is it connected to the land and the temple?

Many of the prayers written by the Diaspora Jews lament the fact that they are waiting for God to bring them back to Zion-Israel. The famous prayer at the end of the *Haggadah* on Passover is stated by every Jew in the world: "Next year in Jerusalem." The daily prayers that Jews throughout the world recite three times a day contain numerous expressions of hope that Jewish people will be returned to Zion. This book will try to detail some of the incongruities with respect to this vitally important subject.

It should be noted that when the king of Persia, Cyrus the Great (590–529 BCE), conquered Babylonia, he expressed his support for Jews returning to the Land of Israel. Despite such overtures, many Jews remained in Babylonia. One can make a case today that the United States is the new Jewish Babylonia and that perhaps the commencement of Jewish guilt stems from the Babylonian Diaspora. It is hoped that after reading this book, Jew and non-Jew alike will have a better understanding of Judaism. Are Jews connected to the land? Or are we waiting until after the Messiah comes to redeem the land?

These are perpetual and emotional questions talked about for the last two thousand years since the destruction of the

Second Temple. Obviously, there are no clear answers.

Like most religions, Judaism provided a way to make amends for sins and to absolve the offender of his guilt. In ancient times, citizens of the Holy Land who sinned against another person or committed a civil wrong could go to the Temple and make a sacrifice, usually a goat. Known as *korban asham*, this guilt was not connected with a sin against God; rather it was for a person-to-person offense, for which the wrongdoer was also expected to make reparations and pay a fine.

In the Diaspora, expiation for the year's sins was addressed in a ritual called *kapparot* the morning before the start of Yom Kippur, the Jewish Day of Atonement, when Jews ask forgiveness from God for their transgressions. In *kapparot*, a chicken to be slaughtered was waved overhead three times. A substitute for one's sins, the chicken was a symbol of divine punishment. While the ritual is maintained in some Hasidic sects, today most Orthodox Jews have replaced the chicken with eighteen cents wrapped in a handkerchief, the number of coins representing the word *chai*, which, in Hebrew, means "alive," the letters of which add up to eighteen.

Among the sins for which Jews are asking forgiveness may be the sin of not obeying the biblical commandment to live in the Holy Land.

As we stated in our book on the *Kaddish*, one of the fundamental bases of Judaism is to study, to learn, and to educate oneself, and the purpose of the rabbis was to encourage study. We also stated in that book that "a spiritual river has many different tributaries and only an individual with extreme hubris would believe that his or her path is the only waterway for truth." That statement certainly applies to the contents of this book. It is quite possible and understandable that certain rabbinical authorities may have a different view of the concept of this book and may disagree with its premise; this ability to disagree is the beauty of Judaism. Questioning authorities and seeking interpretations has been the foundation of Judaic learning. It is axiomatic that in the search for truth and discovery, many different interpretations can be arrived at. We accept and participate in this Jewish principle and thus have written this book with a sense of humility. The Talmud, both Jerusalem and Babylonian, has engendered thousands and thousands of historical thoughts, ideas, and disputes among rabbis and scholars and other highly educated individuals who make it their study. We hope that this book will encourage some who are not familiar with Judaism to study, to analyze, to learn, and perhaps most important, to involve themselves in the process.

PART ONE

· 1 ·

THE MOST DOMINANT BOOK OF
JEWISH LEARNING

$\mathcal{T}$O BEGIN, WE NEED TO ASK: What is the Talmud?
While the question is simple, the answer is not. Philosophically, the Talmud is an unfinished symphony of discourse and commentaries on the body of laws that frame Jewish life. It reads like a discussion across generations conducted by rabbis who pose questions, advance arguments, and, naturally, disagree.

As you might imagine, such a transcription of cross-generational debates does not flow in an obviously logical pattern. Instead it's more like free association. In addition, the editing is not systematic. And although it is spoken of as if it is a single document, there is not one Talmud, but two, each version developed in a distinct geographic location. Moreover, they are written in a mixture of Hebrew and the two dialects of Aramaic that were spoken in early Palestine, which we will call Israel, and in Babylonia, where they were compiled. All these factors are what make it difficult, if not daunting, for the uninitiated student.

The Talmud is not a fictional work, although it contains legends and stories. Nor is it simply a legal work, although it discusses laws and commandments and how they should be observed. It is not an orderly commentary, although it does attempt to interpret the oral and written discourse and traditions of previous generations. Its purpose is not to solve problems or to establish the law, but to record the wisdom of sages past who attempted to resolve questions, thereby facilitating study and setting the stage for future study. It is the religious centerpiece of Judaism, the place where the student can learn about the spiritual and intellectual essence of Judaism. Yet its pages reveal so much more: history, biography, biblical interpretation, philosophy, medicine, botany, astronomy, as well as folklore and superstition.

To understand how this monumental work evolved, let's look at the big picture first. The Bible is the most important document of Jewish literature. The first of its three sections, the Torah (the five books of Moses) is the core of Jewish law. And law—the commandments—is at the heart of Jewish practice. According to tradition, the Torah was revealed to Moses and the Jewish people at Mount Sinai. Yet, from the beginning, questions arose about how to put the law into practice.

The Torah is written in spare language, and Moses and the elders were immediately faced with the need to interpret it and to apply it to their lives. For example, the Fourth Commandment states: "Remember the Sabbath day, to keep it holy" (Exodus 20:8) and goes on to tell us only that no work should be done on that day. So how are we actually supposed to observe the Sabbath? What about feeding the animals? Irrigating the fields? Cooking? All these questions and hundreds more were discussed and expounded upon by generations of elders, scribes, sages, and students. These discussions, passed down orally from generation to generation, formed a body of knowledge that came to be known as the Oral Law. This process of interpreting and expounding is the engine that has powered, and continues to power, Judaism and the Jewish people. It is also the basis of this great work we call the Talmud. In time, the Oral Law, like the Torah on which it was based, began to be thought of as divine revelation.

The Bible—the Torah (the Written Law) and its two other parts, the Prophets and Writings—was completed in about 200 BCE. From that time until about 250 CE, sages referred to as *tannaim* (singular, *tanna*) or "repeaters," studied, taught, and expanded this body of oral commentary and debate. Eventually it became clear that the Oral Law, though previously forbidden to be written down, could no longer remain confined to the memory of the *tannaim*. Geopolitical circumstances, as well as the passage of time, raised the possibility that details of the oral tradition would be forgotten. In addition, the lack of a rational method of resolving disputes, apart from coercion, and the need for a consistent code of law to govern both civic and religious life argued for a permanent document. And so Rabbi Judah Ha-Nasi, who understood the precarious position of Jewish learning in the second century CE, began the process of redacting the Oral Law, which culminated in the construction of the Mishnah. (The word *mishnah* with a lower case *m* also denotes a single paragraph of this collection.)

Because the Mishnah, too, was quite terse and sometimes cryptic, the subsequent five centuries saw the addition of more commentary and discourse to this body of law and discussion. Together with the Mishnah, these additions, the *Gemara* (plural, *gemarot*), which in Aramaic also means "study," form the Talmud. Also included in the Talmud are *baraitot* (singular, *baraita*), external commentary and opinions, which had not been incorporated into the Mishnah.

That two Talmuds were compiled, one in Babylonia and the other in the Land of Israel, is a course of events we will be looking at in detail later. The rabbis responsible for the redaction of the Talmud, the successors to the *tannaim*, were called *amoraim* (singular, *amora*), or "discussers." The sages known as *savoraim* ("expositors") made the amendments and additions that gave the Talmud its final shape.

Let's simplify the picture by making a kind of diagram:

Written Law = The Torah

Oral Law = Orally transmitted commentary on the Torah whose purpose is to explain how to fulfill the Torah's commandments

Mishnah = The codified, written form of the Oral Law.

Gemara = Interpretation and expansion of the Mishnah

Talmud = Mishnah + Gemara[1]

Both the Mishnah and the rest of the Talmud are arranged in the same six Orders[2] and sixty-three *massekhtot* (singular, *massekhet*), tractates or treatises. Although the titles of the Orders and tractates are topics, digressions of all sorts abound. The content of both the Mishnah and Talmud can be divided into two main areas: *halakhah* (law) or the rules that govern Jewish life, which are essentially Torah-based, and *aggadah* (discourse) or any non-*halakhic* Talmudic discussions, more specifically, rabbinic narrative, stories, theological speculation, folklore, and the like.

A body of literature of this sort does not develop in a vacuum. Geopolitical conditions affected the mutability of the Oral Law, thus creating the necessity for writing it down in the first place. Until the era of Judah Ha-Nasi, few had dared attempt such a project. What was going on in Israel during the first and second centuries CE that made this great scholar and politician determine that the bounds of tradition had to be overstepped in order to preserve Judaism?

The history of the Jews up to the second century incorporates the successive empires which ruled over the lands in

---

[1] The Gemara consists of the following: *baraitot* ("bara" means in Aramaic, external; i.e., a Tanaic source external to the Mishnah)—a tradition in one of the Talmuds, attributed to a rabbinic teacher from the time of the Mishnah or even earlier.

Tannaim (repeaters)—the authorities whose work is assembled in the Mishnah.

Amoraim (discussers or expounders)—the rabbinic teachers of the post-Mishnaic era whose traditions are found in the Gemara part of the Talmuds.

Savoraim (expositors)—the rabbis who worked on the final redaction of the Talmud.

Tosefta (supplement)—Tannaitic literature not included in the Mishnah. Arranged in orders and tractates.

[2] The six orders (sedarim) are: *Zraim*—agricultural laws; *Moed*—laws concerning festivals and fasts; *Nashim*—laws relating to women and family life; *Nezikin*—civil and criminal jurisprudence (including the *Pirkei Avot,* ethical teachings); *Kodashim*—laws relating to the Sanctuary and food; *Toharot*— laws of ritual purity.

which they lived, among them Egyptian, Assyrian, Babylonian, Persian, Greek, and Roman. While persecution was
commonplace under all these regimes, the Jews chafed particularly under Roman rule, and a bloody period ensued,
resulting in three major rebellions and the destruction of
the Second Temple in 70 CE (the First Temple had been
destroyed by the Babylonians in 586 BCE). After the great
revolts, Roman repressions made life in the Land of Israel
unstable, and cadres of Torah scholars fled to other countries
or were sold into slavery. This combination of economic
and political instability and ensuing "brain drain" made
it clear that, in the name of preserving the oral traditions
for posterity and future scholarship, they would have to be
written down.

How One Became Two

At the time that the Israeli *amoraim* were compiling the
Talmud, the Jews were affected by the geopolitical vicissitudes
alluded to above, which naturally impacted the development
of Talmudic literature. The ever-increasing pressure they had
to bear under Roman rule, particularly after the fall of the last
Severan emperor, led to their material and spiritual decline.
The subsequent wars of succession undermined the region's
security, and in order to finance these wars, the rulers levied
more and more taxes on the people. This tax burden eroded
the economy of the entire Roman Empire. But the Jews
living in Israel, already devastated by several revolts (mainly
the Great Revolt in the first century of the common era and
the Bar Kokhba Revolt in the second century), were even more
vulnerable to these levies, since most of them were farmers
who could not hide their profits from the authorities.

There was also another factor. The Christians, who had up to then been a persecuted minority, were gaining in strength until, at the beginning of the fourth century, Christianity became the official state religion. It was in this period that Christian persecution of Judaism and Jews began, a harsh blow for the Jews of the Land of Israel. The outcome of this economic decline and political oppression was that Jews emigrated from Israel in droves, scattering to the lands of the Mediterranean Basin, such as Rome itself, Europe, and Babylonia. The academies or yeshivot (singular: yeshiva) of Israel were forced to downsize, and the corps of students diminished. In the fourth generation of *amoraim*, it was already clear that because of the difficult economic situation and lack of opportunities for study, the public was not interested so much in matters of law, preferring instead to focus on legend, which acted as a palliative and was easier to comprehend. This ongoing decline reached such alarming proportions that the sages of Israel were forced to complete the project of compiling what came to be known as the Jerusalem Talmud (*Talmud Yerushalmi*), editing all the Oral Law on hand using any available means.

Outside Israel, Babylonia had been an autonomous Jewish center for longer than any other land, from 586 BCE to 1040 CE, 1,626 years, from the days of the destruction of the First Temple and the Babylonian exile through the Muslim conquest, and up to the Mongol occupation. (Even after its decline, which began in the ninth century, there still remained a vibrant Jewish community in this region of the Middle East, today known as Iraq, until 1948 and shortly thereafter, when the Jews left en masse following the establishment of the State of Israel.)

In contrast to the previous description of the Holy Land's decline under the Romans, Babylonia in the same period was remarkably stable politically and prosperous economically. This atmosphere allowed the Babylonian sages to complete the redaction of their Talmud, which reflects much of the Jerusalem work, with proper care and devotion.

In Babylonia, the most popular method of disseminating Torah learning was through holiday sermons delivered in synagogues by prominent scholars and the heads of the academies. It is interesting to note that women also participated in these public expositions. On these and other occasions, sages would explain legal (*halakhic*) issues, sprinkling their explanations with legends to hold their audience's attention. They delivered their addresses in Hebrew, and a translator would convey their expositions in Aramaic, which was the language of everyday speech. Such translators were also active during the reading of the Torah.

The academies were the focus of study. Aside from the full-time students, who came from wealthy homes, farmers, artisans, and merchants would attend the academy during the slack season. These study methods formed the basis for the written Talmud. Thus the wealth of the land sustained study, the backbone of Judaism and its resilience.

DISTINCTIONS BETWEEN THE JERUSALEM AND BABYLONIAN TALMUDS

Even though the Mishnah is the core of both the Jerusalem and Babylonian Talmuds and similar scholarly methods were used to develop all of this literature, the two Talmuds are quite different in many respects. The most obvious distinction is that the Jerusalem Talmud deals with laws related to Israel and its agriculture, subjects completely absent from the Babylonian text. And even though legend was a popular pursuit in Israel, the Jerusalem work contains much less of this *aggadic* literature than does the Babylonian version. (The Jerusalem's Mishnah even differs in places from the Babylonian one. There is evidence that Rabbi Judah Ha-Nasi changed single verses, writing them in two different versions.)

The two Talmuds also do not contain the same number of tractates. Although both are arranged according to the six Orders of the Mishnah—(1) *Zraim*, agricultural laws; (2) *Moed*, laws concerning festivals and fasts; (3) *Nashim*, laws relating to woman and family life; (4) *Nezikin*, civil and criminal jurisprudence; (5) *Kodashim*, laws relating to the Sanctuary and food; and (6) *Toharot*, laws of ritual purity—not every tractate of the Mishnah has a completion or *gemara*. The Babylonian Talmud has *gemarot* for only thirty-six tractates. In the first Order, *Zraim* (seeds), there is a *gemara* only for *Berakhot* (blessings), but not for the other tractates, which deal with laws concerning the Land of Israel and its agriculture in the period prior to the destruction of the Temple. In addition, in the last Order, *Toharot* (purities), there is a *gemara* for only one tractate, *Niddah* (menstruation). The *amoraim* of Babylonia wrote *gemarot* for these tractates as well, but they were lost because they were not a focus of study.

The Jerusalem Talmud has a *gemara* just for the first four Orders (with small omissions), including the entire Order of *Zraim* and for forty tractates altogether. In contrast, the Babylonian Talmud does not have a *gemara* for the Orders *Kodashim* and *Toharot* (aside from a few sections), although it seems that they were composed at the time, only to be lost later. In fact, the Babylonian Talmud is about four times as large as the Jerusalem, consisting of 5,894 folio pages.

The Jerusalem *talmud* contains an amoraic on *massekhet Shkalim* (tractate on money), which is missing in the Babylonian. However the entire *Seder Kodashim*, the fifth Order of the Mishnah in the Jerusalem Talmud, is now lost, although it is believed that some scholars, including the great medieval philosopher and scholar Maimonides, had managed to see and use it. Several more chapters from the Jerusalem are lost as well, such as the final seven chapters of *massekhet Niddah* (tractate on women and the family) and chapter three of *massekhet Makot* (a tractate on punishment).

Negotiations, which are plentiful in the Babylonian, do not exist in the Jerusalem Talmud. The Babylonian Talmud dwelt on every phrase that was not clear and interpreted it, whereas the Jerusalem Talmud did not. The Babylonian alone also tried to solve the contradictions between the beginnings and the endings in the Mishnah. Apparently the first sages did have many of the Mishnah *massekhtot* (tractates), which are now lost.

While the *halakhic* part in the Babylonian is clearer than the Jerusalem's, the *aggadot*, the legends, in the Jerusalem are easier to understand than in the Babylonian. In the Jerusalem, they are written simply, while in the Babylonian they are sometimes described in flowery language, which makes comprehension more difficult. Even so, sometimes we find *aggadot* in the Babylonian whose source is in the Jerusalem and vice versa.

What is even more obvious is the lack of editing in the Jerusalem work. It is a much more transparent reflection of the oral tradition from which it sprang. It is largely unedited and resembles a debate with stream-of-consciousness argumentation, which makes it more obtuse and difficult to follow than its Babylonian relation. It lacks the precision of that text, which was revised over a longer period of time and with greater care.

Work on the Jerusalem Talmud ended a long time before its correlate in Babylonia because of the troubles in the Land of Israel and the thinning out of the population during the era of Byzantine rule there in the early Middle Ages. Without the necessary time required to edit the work properly, its redaction was nevertheless completed in 420 CE. This is one reason why it came to be considered the stepbrother of the Babylonian Talmud. Furthermore, the Babylonian text may have been accorded more authority over the years because it developed over a longer period of time and is more complete, in addition to leaving more room for further scholarship and interpretation. Since the *amoraim* who compiled the Babylonian Talmud were not working under duress, they concluded their redaction 140 years after their Israeli counterparts. The fact that the Babylonian text was completed later was the reason that the medieval sages decided that if a difference of opinion arose between the two Talmuds, the Babylonian would take precedence.

The Mishnah is written in Hebrew, although it also contains Greek and Latin words and expressions. In the centuries following its redaction, Aramaic became the vernacular in both Israel and Babylonia. Aramaic, which was in use for over three thousand years, beginning in the eleventh century BCE, is closer to Hebrew than any other Semitic language. During the late Assyrian and Persian kingdoms (sixth century BCE), international commerce was conducted in Aramaic. In Israel, where it was the lingua franca for centuries, the Bible was translated into Aramaic in synagogues. Many prayers recited today, including the *Kaddish*, are in Aramaic. Prayers, liturgical poetry, and texts, such as the *Zohar* (works of mystical commentary on the Torah), were also written in Aramaic even after it was no longer spoken.

So the four generations of *amoraim* who compiled the Gemara of Israel, mainly in the Galilee, and the eight generations of *amoraim* who worked on the Babylonian version, mainly in the yeshivas of Nehardea, Sura, and Pumbedita, spoke and wrote Aramaic. But each Talmud is written in a different dialect of Aramaic. Thus the Jerusalem Talmud is composed in Western Aramaic (Syriac), which closely resembles the biblical Aramaic of parts of the books Ezra and Daniel, whereas the Babylonian Talmud is written in the Eastern Aramaic dialect used there.

Incidentally, it is worth noting that what we call the Jerusalem Talmud was not actually written down in Jerusalem at all, since Jews were prohibited from living in or even entering their ancient capital, which had become a pagan city called Aelia Capitolina. Over the centuries, however, Jerusalem became synonymous with the Land of Israel, and therefore the Talmud that was created there, apparently in Tiberias and partly in Caesarea, is known as the Jerusalem Talmud.

Interest in the Jerusalem Talmud, which was never the subject of mainstream study, has been renewed only in the past few centuries. This revitalization reflects the trend toward gleaning from the Talmudic text information about the cultures in which its authors lived, their attitudes, and their interests. To this end, modern scholars sometimes compare parallel passages in both Talmuds. Nevertheless, the Babylonian version is still considered the richer of the two, although more skill is required to study it. It contains multiple, parallel arguments and commentaries on the *mishnah* under discussion, along with references and links to other parts of the text and other sources, similar in a way to today's hypertext. In general, the Babylonian Talmud is of greater legal significance than the Jerusalem Talmud and is a more complete work.

The two Talmuds developed in the most outstanding Talmudic academies or yeshivas of the two Torah centers, Israel and Babylonia. In fact, it seems that there was much collaboration between them. So long as the Israeli yeshivas existed, the sages of both lands, Babylonia and Israel, were in constant contact and an interchange of ideas flowed in both directions. Many of the Israeli sages were sent to Babylonia to study its academies' methods of instruction; they were called *nachoti* (those who "descended" to Babylonia), in contrast to *olim* (those who "make *aliyah*" or "ascend" to Israel). On the other hand, many Babylonian sages would go up to Israel from time to time to learn about ancient laws, which had been traditions from the days of the *tannaim*.

In Israel, the home of the *tannaim*, these traditions as well as the original versions of sections of the Mishnah were better preserved than in Babylonia. In this way, the words of the Babylonian sages were published in Israel and vice versa. This is also why we find most of the discourse of the Israeli sages in the Babylonian Talmud and why Rabbi Yochanan, the redactor of the Jerusalem Talmud, and his colleague Resh Lakish figure prominently in the Babylonian Talmud.

By the same token, much of what was discussed by the Babylonian sages is found in the Jerusalem Talmud, particularly the teachings of Rav and Shmuel, the fathers of the Babylonian Talmud.

We will discuss more about these sages in the next chapter.

Of course, interpretation did not stop with the completion of these manuscripts. It continues to this very day. Rabbinic authorities have continued to grapple with ambiguities and the questions these generate throughout the generations. As long as they continue to answer these questions, creating interpretations and commentary, then Jewish scholarship will continue. Some of the better-known commentators on the Talmud are Rashi (Rabbi Shlomo Yitzhaki) in medieval France (1040–1105), Maimonides in Spain, Morocco, and later Egypt (1135–1204), and others from the Middle Ages. Later on, the idea of codifying law (*halakhah*), separating it from discourse (*aggadah*), was taken up by Maimonides, Rabbi Yoseph Karo (author of the *Shulhan Aruch*), and others. The *responsa* literature—questions addressed to great rabbis and their responses—which were collected down the ages, also provide interpretations of law based on these texts.

· 2 ·

WHO'S WHO IN EACH TALMUD?

THE *AMORAIM*

After the Mishnah was concluded, and some time after the death of Rabbi Judah Ha-Nasi (who is known simply as Rabbi), a new period began in the history of the Oral Law, the period of the Mishnah explainers or interpreters, called the *amoraim*. *Amora* means "interpreter" or "translator" or "expounder." This title reflects a certain role which was created in the time of the *tannaim* when the scholar would sit on a stage and discuss matters of the *halakhah* and *aggadah* and talk to the public in Hebrew. His younger pupils would repeat his words loudly in Aramaic. They did the same during the public reading of the Torah, so that it would be understood by all. The *amoraim* were therefore both translators and at times also popularizers of the basic *halakhah* issues discussed by the scholars.

The generations immediately following Rabbi's death acted as an interim time between the *tannaim* ("repeaters," whose views are included in the Mishnah) and the *amoraim* (whose views are included in the Talmud), continuing the study and explanation work of the Mishnah. The reason for this gap probably was the absence of a single leading scholar. Rabbi Judah Ha-Nasi handed down his position as president of the Sanhedrin, the Jewish court, to his firstborn, Raban Gamliel, who was morally a distinguished personality but certainly not the greatest scholar of his generation. The role of the head of the yeshiva was given to Rabbi Hanina.

From that time forward, the Sanhedrin presidency became a politically prestigious position, but not the leading scholarly one it had been when the Sanhedrin presidents also served as presidents of the School of Hillel for the *tannaim* (founded by Hillel the Elder).

This separation bore new yeshivas, which were established by great scholars such as Rabbi Hiyya, Rabbi Oshaya, and others. His pupils and close friends who lived in the interim period of the *tannaim* and the *amoraim* continued the work Rabbi (Ha-Nasi) had begun, compiling and arranging materials from the previous generations which they thought worthy of preserving for purposes of comparison and interpretation of the Mishnah. Thus Rabbi Hiyya and Rabbi Oshaya, who had been Rabbi's celebrated pupils, gathered and arranged several additional compilations which now comprise a book named *Tosefta*. *Tosefta* is an Aramaic word meaning an "addition," and the book is a supplement to the Mishnah. This book also is a concise formulation of the Oral Law based on the method devised by Rabbi Nehemia, a disciple of the famous Rabbi Akiva, a renowned sage and contributor to the Mishnah. The explanations, called *midrashim* (singular: *midrash*), of the *halakhah* highlight the link between the Written and the Oral Torah, which were compiled and arranged mainly during these years.

Other scholars continued to prepare additional compilations of material that belonged to the *tannaim*, but few survived through time. Single *halakhah* and the compilations of *tannaitic* material which were *external* to the Mishnah were called *baraitot* (singular: *baraita*), meaning that these paragraphs were not an actual part of the Mishnah. This abundant material of the *tosaftot* (additions) was named by these generations "eighty mistresses," while the Mishnah's *massakhtot* (the tractates or discussions) were named "sixty queens" and the *halakhot* (the laws) were the "maidens."

However, only in the second generation after Rabbi Judah Ha-Nasi did genuine *amoraic* scholarly activity begin, and various scholars continued to establish centers throughout Israel: in Lod and Ceasaria, and in Zippori, which became the traditional opponent of the yeshiva in Tiberias.

This great work of compilation and preservation continued for several more generations, but its importance declined because the main direction of Torah study had changed its course. The conclusion of the Mishnah period coincided with the rise of the Babylonian independent Torah center, although there had been scholars in Babylonia during all the generations, and some of the greatest *tannaim* such as Hillel Ha-Zaken had come from there. However, it had always been a branch of the Israeli Torah. With the death of Rabbi

Judah Ha-Nasi, this emphasis began to change, and the first seeds of guilt were planted.

THE BABYLONIAN *AMORAIM*

The fact that Rabbi had no successor distinctly weakened the influence of Israel. That, combined with the deterioration of the political and economical state of the Israeli Jews, prompted many to move elsewhere. The fragility of the Israeli influence opened an opportunity to establish a spiritual center in Babylonia, the strength of which eventually eclipsed that of Israel. This was done by Abba Arikha ("tall" Abba), who had come to Israel from Babylonia as a young man with his uncle Rabbi Hiyya, a pupil and friend of Rabbi Judah Ha-Nasi. Abba Arikha lived in Israel for many years studying at Rabbi's yeshiva, where he was considered a brilliant scholar, and he was so respected by his generation's elders and sages that they consulted him over regulations. He was ordained by Rabbi Judah Ha-Nasi and was well versed in the teachings of both the Babylonian and Israeli scholars. He traveled back and forth between Israel and Babylonia several times, eventually choosing to settle in Babylonia, where he was needed.

When Abba Arikha arrived in Babylonia, he found that even though there were important young scholars there, the Torah study was fragmented and of a low level. There was no academy or yeshiva in the area, only a reading of the weekly portion from the five books of Moses, in the local house of prayer or study hall. Not wanting to offend the existing leadership, he decided to settle in the small town of Sura, where he put up his yeshiva, an academy that rather quickly became an important center of Torah studies, one that lasted for seven hundred years. Abba Arikha was so influential in Babylonia that they called him "Rav" rather than by his own name, and that is how he has been known ever since.

The title Rav came about because, according to the *halakhah*, it was impossible to give a formal ordination to scholars outside the Land of Israel. Since the Babylonian scholars could not be called "Rabbi," they received the title "Rav," which attested to their degree of knowledge but did not qualify them formally and authoritatively.

One of the greatest scholars of his generation, Rav made his living from international trade and was also known as a holy and generous man. He inspired his cousin Shmuel to take up the leadership of another yeshiva in the town of Nehardea, which became a friendly competitor to the yeshiva in Sura.

Rav and Shmuel together were the first generation of the Babylonian *amoraim* who shaped the new fashion of the Torah study for the subsequent generations. They were close friends though completely different from each other. Rav's family descended from King David, and he was related through marriage to the exilarch or head of the exiled community (*Rosh Hagola*). He personified the tradition of studying that had been cultivated in Israel and was editor of some compilations of verses in the Mishnah. In his Bet Midrash (a rabbinical school, literally "House of Interpretation," and by extension House of Learning), the legal interpretation for the book of Vayikra (Leviticus) was arranged in its final shape and was indeed called "the book of Bet Rav" or "the book of the house of Rav." Rav Abba Arikha also composed some of the main prayers for Rosh Hashanah.

Shmuel was one of the important physicians of his generation as well as a great astronomer, and he served as the *av bet din*, chief justice of the Jewish court in Babylonia. Both their yeshivas developed a study method that dealt with the explanation of the Mishnah, aided by parallel sources from the external *mishnayot*, looking at the verses from all possible sides.

The two large yeshivas concentrated on the study of the Mishnah and its comprehensive research. Naturally there were many differences in their attitudes, and discussions between Rav and Shmuel became foundations for study in that generation and the next one. Such was their influence that the following generation ruled that in financial matters, the *halakhah* was to be according to the interpretations of Shmuel, and in other matters, according to Rav's.

After the time of Rav and Shmuel, many Babylonian scholars immigrated to the Holy Land, where they were highly respected. However, the Babylonian yeshivas were already important and had established their own independent schools of thought. Rav was succeeded in Sura by his pupil Rav Huna. And Shmuel was succeeded by Rav Yehuda, who was also Rav's pupil and who moved the yeshiva in Nehardea, which was situated on the Persian-Roman border, to Pumbedita.

The famous scholars of these generations also included Rav Hisda; the blind but extremely knowledgeable Rav Sheshet, called the "iron man"; Rav Nachman, who was a brilliant judge; and many others.

In the third generation of the *amoraim*, another pair of scholars stood out: One was Rabbah, short for Rav Abba bar Nachmani, who was extremely clever and amiable and was nicknamed *Oker Harim* or "mountains extractor" by his fellow scholars; he became the head of the Pumbedita Yeshiva at a very young age. Another was Rav Yoseph, called "Sinai," who became blind in old age and succeeded his friend Rabbah as head of the yeshiva. Their points of view became part of the curriculum of the yeshivas.

In addition to the Babylonian scholars, there were scholars who also taught the Torah teaching of Israel, and this renewed influence bore its fruit with the pillars of the Babylonian Torah, Abbaye and Rava.

Abbaye is the name Rav Abba gave his nephew Nachmani ben Kaylil ("Abbaye" probably means "a small father"). Abbaye, who was an orphan, grew up at his uncle's home and made his living as a farmer. He studied under his uncle and Rav Yoseph, whom he later criticized strongly. Eventually he succeeded Rav Yoseph as head of the yeshiva. Abbaye's partner Rava (Abba ben Rav Hama) studied in another school, that of Rav Nachman and Rav Hisda. He was a successful merchant and close to the Persian Court and lived in the rich trading town of Mahoza. The two men were good friends though they differed greatly in their opinions. Their disputes, called *Havayot d'Abbayei ve Rabba*, appear frequently in the Babylonian Talmud, and the clarifications of their opinions exemplify the classical study of the Babylonian Talmud. Both scholars were very clever and knowledgeable, with Abbaye predisposed to formalism and Rava to realism. Abbaye's conclusions tended to be simple solutions, while Rava was quicker with his decisions but they involved more complex thought-structures. Despite their differences, they established many *halakhic* elements through joint work.

Their contributions were so vast and deep that the next generation's scholars, Rav Papa and Rav Papi, Rav Nachman

Bar Yizhak and Rav Huna, dealt mainly with the development of their work and the conclusions drawn from it. In fact it was recognized that the Abbaye and Rava period was a turning point in the study of the Torah. Before them, the oral tradition "out of the mouth of the teachers" was central in this study; with them it began to be based more on analysis and criticism, self-research and placement of methods. Therefore the *halakhah* of the later generations is more important than that of the previous ones.

In the sixth generation of the Babylonian *amoraim*, another great personality appeared on the stage. Rav Ashi, head of Sura Yeshiva, was the political leader of the Jewish people in Babylonia. A well-to-do man who was close to the Persian rulers and thus even more powerful than the head of the exiled community (Rosh Hagola), Rav Ashi was the greatest scholar of his generation. His combination of wisdom and power, like that of Rabbi Judah Ha-Nasi, allowed him to address an enormous problem that had evolved—the wealth of material to study that had accumulated over the ages and that was in danger of getting lost unless it was sorted out and arranged. Rav Ashi was driven to edit the Babylonian Talmud. This was a huge enterprise, even greater than the Mishnah's arrangement. Although his own name does not appear frequently in the Talmud, much of the anonymous material is his own. It is believed that this huge task was not done by Rav Ashi alone; his pupil, friend, and successor Rabina continued it. These two scholars are considered by many to be the final *amoraim*.

In the next hundred years, scholars who were called *savoraim* (singular: *savora*), meaning "expositors," continued to study the Talmud, adding to it and giving it its final version.

We do not name a person who concluded the Talmud, and therefore it is said that it has not been finished. Actually it has never really stopped being created through all the following generations.

The Israeli *Amoraim*

The Golden Age of the Talmud in Israel is linked with one personality who established a center of the Israeli Torah: Rabbi Yochanan, who was also called Bar Nafcha, the blacksmith's son. He was a student of Rabbi Yanai and Hizkiya ben Rabbi Hiyya, as well as one of Rabbi Judah Ha-Nasi's younger students.

Rabbi Yochanan was born in the Lower Galilee in the town of Zippori, also the home at that time to Rabbi Judah Ha-Nasi. Rabbi Yochanan's father died before he was born, and soon after his birth his mother died as well. He was raised by his grandfather. As a child he was noted for his strong memory. He attended Rabbi's lessons but only as a junior student. As an adult, he had some knowledge of science and medicine.

His father left him an inheritance of fields and vineyards between Zippori and Tiberias, but Yochanan sold them all in order to dedicate himself to the study of the Torah. He spent all his time studying the Torah and was known to say that walking idly without studying should be considered blasphemous. According to one story about him, he was strolling with his pupil Rabbi Hiyya bar Abba in the fields and he pointed to them saying: "All these were mine and I've sold them in order to study the Torah." Rabbi Hiyya was said to weep at hearing that his mentor was left with nothing. Rabbi Yochanan calmed him by explaining: "My son

Hiyya, I sold something that was given for six days during which they (the fields) were created by God, and bought the Torah which was given for forty days."

Rabbi Yochanan was famous for his humane outlook and good deeds, and stories illustrating these traits were sewn into both Talmuds. He also was an exceptionally good-looking man. He was described as having the beauty of a silver glass filled with red pomegranate kernels, its rims surrounded by red roses, which is placed between the sunlight and the shade. He would sit at the entrance of the ritual bath so that the daughters of Israel who came to purify themselves could look at him and give birth to handsome boys. When asked if he was not afraid of the Evil Eye, he answered, "No, I am a descendant of Joseph, who was not given to the Evil Eye."

After teaching in Zippori, Rabbi Yochanan saw the need to establish a central yeshiva. However, he didn't want to offend Rabbi Judah Ha-Nasi by setting up one in Zippori, so he moved to Tiberias. His yeshiva there attracted thousands of students, among whom were some of the great *amoraim* of the second and third generations, in both Israel and Babylonia. Forty-eight *amoraim* came from Babylonia to his yeshiva in Tiberias to study with him and most of them returned to Babylonia afterwards. Thanks to his students, his *halakhot* and statements fill the Babylonian Talmud. After the death of Rav and Shmuel in Babylonia, Rabbi Yochanan remained the greatest of his generation both in Israel and in Babylonia.

Rabbi Yochanan loved Israel with all his heart, and he never left it, although he once considered visiting Shmuel in Babylonia before he learned of Shmuel's death. He said of the Holy Land: "He who walks *dalet amot* [the established reach of a person] in Israel, *Olam Haba* [afterlife] is promised to him." (*Dalet* is the fourth letter of the Hebrew alphabet. So, Rabbi Yochanan meant that if a man walked only four feet in the Land of Israel, it would be sufficient to qualify him for the afterlife.) He also said: "Better eat everyday a slice of bread and salt (in Israel) than live in a house filled with meat and thefts," and "Jerusalem will become the capital of all countries."

Rabbi Yochanan was also famous for his love of people: "Hospitality is greater than getting up early to go to the study hall," and also "Visiting the sick, Hospitality, and Judging contribute [on Judgment Day] to a lenient view." However, his personal life was extremely unhappy. All his arduous studies did not save him from suffering. His ten sons died during his lifetime, and because he devoted his life to his work, he gradually lost all his property. Nevertheless, he headed the Tiberias Yeshiva for sixty years, and because of him, the Israeli Torah flourished.

Rabbi Yochanan lived to almost 100 and saw the end of the first generation of the Israeli *amoraim* and the beginning of the third generation. During his lifetime the Tiberias Yeshiva became the greatest center in the world for the study of the Oral Torah. A letter from Israel would often solve disputes among Babylonian scholars, and Rabbi Yochanan's opinions took precedence even against the joint opinions of Rav and Shmuel.

Rabbi Yochanan is also credited with a unique historical deed: the codification of the Jerusalem Talmud, which is known by several other names as well—Talmud Yerushalmi, Talmud Eretz Israel, and *Talmuda Di'vney Ma'arava* (the Westerners' Talmud in Aramaic). The medieval sage Mai-

monides, in his introduction to the explanation of the Mishnah, says: "And so did the Scholars of Israel, like Rav Ashi,
they wrote the Jerusalem Talmud and Rabbi Yochanan is
the author." This does not mean that Rabbi Yochanan completed the Jerusalem Talmud, because many of the scholars
mentioned in the Jerusalem Talmud lived after Yochanan;
it means that Rabbi Yochanan edited the Jerusalem Talmud
in Tiberias, and the pupils who followed him completed it.
Similarly, the Babylonian Talmud was edited by Rav Ashi,
and succeeding rabbis completed it later.

During the many years of Rabbi Yochanan's position as
head of the yeshiva, he developed special study methods for
Israel. Though he was well versed in and appreciative of the
Babylonian scholars, he had his own method of teaching.
Generally, the Israeli tendency was to explain issues in a
more simplistic way than in Babylonia. This approach was
due to their confidence in their power and in the fact that
the Israeli scholars were entitled to determine basic *halakhot*
on their own without the need to try to interpret the Mishnah in a forced and complex way.

Rabbi Yochanan's rules for determining the way things
should be were unequivocal, and he tended to find a uniform
way of interpreting the various paragraphs (*mishnayot*) in the
Mishnah using his enormous knowledge and analytical gift.
In addition, his study methods and personality not only gave
him authority over the Israeli scholars but also attracted
Babylonian scholars, who began to consider him the teacher
of the entire generation. Many of the important *amoraim* in
Babylonia decided to move to Israel in order to study with
him, thus becoming fervent admirers of the local method
of study. One of these newcomers was the bright Rav Kah-

ana, Rav's student, and others including Rabbi Eleazar ben Pedat, Rav Ami, Rav Asi, and more. Of course all the local scholars considered themselves his pupils as well. However, his closest scholar and friend was Rabbi Simeon ben Lakish, who was known as Resh Lakish.

Resh Lakish was born to a poor family in Zippori, ten years after Rabbi Yochanan. In his youth, he was not a Torah student. Instead, forced to make a living (this is mentioned only in the Babylonian Talmud), he joined the people of Lydia, who were known for their archery. The Romans had built circuses and stadiums there, as well as schools for training boxers. These athletes, some of whom were criminals, were well fed to keep them fit. Resh Lakish became a circus gladiator. Some think he joined them, planning to rescue the Jewish slaves among the boxers, but he was a gladiator only for a short time. Thanks to his physical strength, he managed to survive his battles. He was rescued through a romantic episode, a dramatic meeting with Rabbi Yochanan that changed his life.

The story goes that Rabbi Yochanan saw Resh Lakish bathing in the Jordan River. Impressed by the man's athletic body, he told him "your force—to the Torah." Resh Lakish, who admired Rabbi Yochanan's unusual handsomeness, replied "your beauty—to the women." Then Rabbi Yochanan told Lakish that he had a sister more beautiful than he was and promised to give his pretty sister to Resh Lakish as a wife if he would abandon his occupation as gladiator and immerse himself in the study of the Torah. And indeed that is what happened. Rabbi Yochanan let Resh Lakish marry his sister and became both his brother-in-law and favorite teacher. And Resh

Lakish fulfilled his side of the bargain by becoming one of the greatest scholars of his generation.

Resh Lakish was a charitable person, who supported himself as an orchard guard and was never worried about his next meal. Witty and sharp and a diligent student, he demanded these qualities from others as well, saying that "the words of Torah are realized only in he who kills himself over it." He also became an ascetic, never laughing or speaking with a person suspected of dishonesty. It was said that whoever has a conversation with Resh Lakish is so reliable that one could lend him money without witnesses. Yet Lakish himself was so poor that his only possessions found after his death were a small number of crocuses, which were used in the preparation of yellow coloring.

Resh Lakish died before Rabbi Yochanan, and the latter, blaming himself, passed away a short while after. One story says the two had a disagreement over the question of finishing off the fabrication of weapons. Rabbi Yochanan reminded Resh Lakish that he should know about weapons from his days in Lydia. Resh Lakish became enraged, and the violent emotion was blamed for his death. Distraught, Rabbi Yochanan screamed his heart out: "Bar Lakisha, where are you?" He kept on screaming until he lost his mind. His students and colleagues implored God to have mercy on Rabbi Yochanan and to relieve him of his madness, and he expired.

The analytical arguments between Rabbi Yochanan and Resh Lakish are many. Rabbi Yochanan considered them the most complete way to develop the Torah, and when Resh Lakish was absent, Rabbi Yochanan said of himself that he was like a man who tries clapping with one hand.

More than 3,000 *amoraim* are mentioned by their names

in both Talmuds; all the rest are anonymous. The *amoraim* who appear in the Jerusalem Talmud and its other authors also took part in the writing of the Babylonian Talmud. The Babylonian *amoraim* are mentioned in the Jerusalem version as well. The Talmud sages sat in the large Torah study centers in Israel—Tiberias, Zippori, and Keysarin—and in Babylonia—Nehardea, Sura, Mahoza, and Pumbedita.

In order to establish a firm contact with the Israeli Torah, a special role was created, that of the *nachoti* (literally, the descenders)—scholars who came down from the Holy Land to Babylonia to deliver news from the Tiberias Yeshiva. Some of the *nachoti* were merchants who needed to be in Babylonia for their trade connections, but most of them were messengers from the Tiberias Yeshiva who were sent there especially for this purpose, and also to obtain financial support for the institution, perhaps relying on the guilt of the Babylonians in their more affluent communities to induce generous donations.

In some generations, the heads of the yeshivas were very rich people or they would receive large sums of money from the public to maintain them and support their students. The larger yeshivas were granted grounds and buildings. The permanent students were only a small part of the audience of Torah learners. A larger part attended the institution called *Yarchei Kala*, a so-called "popular university" that Jewish Babylonia arranged twice a year in the months of Adar and Elul (collectively called Kala), when field work was relatively scant. Thousands of people, all eager to hear and study the Torah, would gather in the yeshivas to learn from the heads of the academies.

In each of these months one verse (*massekhet*) of the Mishnah was publicly studied and another was "exposed" or revealed and generally explained for the next month of studies, so that the scholars could study the new verse to prepare for its public discussion.

The head of the yeshiva would sit at the top of the hall. Next to him were the important scholars—his best pupils and some friends—followed by all the other students. In Israel and in the more public yeshivas, the seating order followed a very strict hierarchy, according to scholarly importance that was preserved from the period of the Sanhedrin.

In the lesson, the head of the yeshiva would present an interpretation of a certain problem. Sometimes the students would confront him with questions based on other opinions and sources. At other times, additional scholars would offer alternative solutions, resulting in a multiparticipant debate. The head of the yeshiva, who acted as chairman, would sum up the discussion or would support a certain opinion. The solutions would be delivered to other yeshivas and scholars, who would study and comment on them during the year. Then this additional material would be added to the previously determined opinions.

Because the debates and study were rather intensive and composed mainly of opinions exchanged among the important scholars in the yeshiva, not all the learners would be able to follow and remember them. Therefore, after the fixed month of study, there would be additional sessions of revision and preparation, directed not by the head of the yeshiva but by a special person who was called *Rosh Kala* (literally: the head of the time of Kala). He would explain and extend the things said and revise their meaning with the learners. The Rosh Kala were considered seconds to the heads of the yeshiva, and some of them eventually became heads of the yeshivas themselves. They were closer to the audience, and at times they developed special friendships with their students. Some think that the blessing in Aramaic, *Yekum Purkan*, which was introduced into the Ashkenazi prayerbook, was at first a version of the pupils' blessings and farewell from the Rosh Kala.

The length of the *amoraim* period was 160 years (219–359). The Jerusalem Talmud was codified 160 years before the codifying of the Babylonian Talmud, and, as was pointed out earlier, because the Babylonian version came later, every time there was a dispute with the Jerusalem version over a certain interpretation of law, the Babylonian teaching prevailed.

· 3 ·

The Issue of the Inheritance of Israel and Its Sacredness

To understand the genesis of the friction between the Israeli and Babylonian communities, the presumptive source of Jewish guilt, we need to look at the biblical imperative to live in the Land of Israel. The roots of the Jewish people in the Holy Land are embedded in the biblical promise of the land to our forefathers. The promises given to Abraham are found in Genesis 13:14–15, 17.

> *14: And the* Lord *said unto Abram, Lift up now thine eyes, and look from the place where thou art northward, and southward, and eastward, and westward:*

15: For all the land which thou seest, to thee will I give it, and to thy seed for ever.

17: Arise, walk through the land in the length of it and in the breadth of it; for I will give it unto thee.

It is also expressed in the *Brith beyn Habtarim* (Covenant between the Pieces) in Genesis 15:7:

7: And he said unto him, I am the LORD *that brought thee out of Ur of the Chaldees, to give thee this land to inherit it.*

Immediately after that, Abraham asks the Lord: GOD, whereby shall I know that I shall inherit it? And the Spanish Talmudist Nachmanides, who is known as Ramban (a Hebrew acronym for Rabbi Moshe ben Nachman), explains Abraham's question with regard to the inheritance of Israel by the People of Israel, as follows: Abraham was concerned that the People of Israel could inherit the land only if they behaved according to the Torah; however, he wasn't asking God for a sign to ensure this inheritance, but rather expressing his own worry in case his own or his descendants' sins would prevent it. And indeed the Lord assured him that this inheritance would be enacted according to the covenant made between them and would be given to the seed of Abraham for an "everlasting possession." This idea is repeated in Deutronomy 9:4.

When the Lord commands Abraham and his descendants to be circumcised as a token of the covenant with God, he repeats the promise of the inheritance of the land in Genesis 17:8:

8: And I will give unto thee, and to thy seed after thee, the land wherein thou art a stranger, all the land of Canaan, for an everlasting possession; and I will be their God.

Ramban followed his own interpretation to verse 8 and explained the expression "everlasting possession" to mean that if they were exiled from the land (because of their sins), they would return and repossess it.

The promise to Isaac is expressed in Genesis 26:2–4:

2: And the LORD *appeared unto him, and said, Go not down into Egypt; dwell in the land which I shall tell thee of:*

3: Sojourn in this land, and I will be with thee, and will bless thee; for unto thee, and unto thy seed, I will give all these countries, and I will perform the oath which I swore unto Abraham thy father;

4: And I will make thy seed to multiply as the stars of heaven, and will give unto thy seed all these countries; and in thy seed shall all the nations of the earth be blessed;

Hayyim ben Moses Attar, known as Or Ha-Chayim or "Light of Lights" (1696–1743), a Sephardi interpreter who was accepted in the Ashkenazi Hasidic circles, explained these verses: God wanted to promise Abraham that Yishmael will have no part in the promise to Abraham; it was intended for Isaac only, as was explicitly said in Genesis 21:12: "for in Isaac shall thy seed be called." Since Abraham had two sons it had to be explicitly stated which son would inherit the land.

The Promises to Jacob

When Isaac parts from Jacob, his son who flees from his brother Esau to Laban, he blesses him in Genesis 28:4

4: And give thee the blessing of Abraham, to thee, and to thy seed with thee; that thou mayest inherit the land wherein thou art a stranger, which God gave unto Abraham.

The fleeing Jacob dreams "and behold a ladder set up on the earth," and then God is revealed to him:

> *13: And, behold, the LORD stood above it, and said, I am the LORD God of Abraham thy father, and the God of Isaac: the land whereon thou liest, to thee will I give it, and to thy seed.*

The medieval French scholar Rabbi Shlomo Yitzhaki (1040–1105), known by the Hebrew acronym Rashi, interprets "the land whereon thou liest" to mean that the Lord folded the entire Israel under Jacob to the size of a human volume, thus hinting that it will be easy for his sons to conquer it.

The verse from Genesis 35:12, "And the land which I gave Abraham and Isaac, to thee I will give it, and to thy seed after thee will I give the land," is interpreted by Ramban as: I gave them; I shall give it to you as well. I gave it to them upon my oath to Abraham and Yitzchak [Isaac] and therefore it is an absolute giving independently of the behavior of the sons of Israel [Jacob].

Or Ha-Chayim notes the double mention of God's promise to give the land: "To thee I will give it" and then "I shall give it to you."

The promises to the People of Israel are unequivocal and appear several times, in Exodus 6, in Psalms 105:11, and elsewhere. On the everlasting link between the People of Israel, the Torah of Israel, and the Land of Israel, it was said that the Lord matched Israel to the People of Israel (*Bamidbar Raba* 27:5–7). There are many mentions of this, among them one from Ramban, who says that one should know that the Land of Israel is worthy of the People of Israel and is its patrimony, and he refers to Deutronomy 32:8: "When the most High divided to the nations their inheritance, when he separated the sons of Adam, he set the bounds of the people according to the number of the children of Israel."

The Maggid (preacher) of Dubna in *Kol Bokhim*, which means "weeping voice," explains the idea in his special way, by an allegory:

You should know that our sacred land was not like the rest of the nations. Their lands serve them as a residence place only and have no particular traits; however the Land of Israel has special traits for the People of Israel and only for them, and it is exactly like the garment which is made to fit a certain person and no other, unless he will spoil it by altering its size, etc. So was Israel specially fitted for the People of Israel.

According to the Judaic view, Israel is the place of the Divine Presence, a fact that constitutes the basis for the match of the Land to the People. The same fact makes it the holiest land of all lands.

Only in Israel—the place of the Divine Presence—can the uniqueness of the People of Israel be expressed. This idea is stressed in Rabbi Yehuda Halevi's book *Ha-Kuzari*, in chapter 2:10–12:

> *Don't be surprised by the fact that a certain land will have an advantage over the others, since there are differences between the lands in their flora, fauna, and natural resources, and in the characteristics of its people. However, Israel is the land which is capable of achieving the chief spiritual advantage [which is the prophecy from the Divine linkage] for the* Am Segula, *Unique People, who are like the heart and soul of all the nations. Also, it is not possible for this Unique People to obtain the Divine Abundance in a place other than the Land of Israel.*

THE OBSERVANCE OF THE MITZVOT OF THE TORAH—
ONLY IN THE LAND OF ISRAEL

Quite a few sources tell us that there is an inseparable link between the people of Israel, the Torah, and the Land of Israel. Deutronomy 11:17 says that if the People of Israel do not observe the Torah and its commandments, they will ... *perish quickly from off the good land which the* LORD *giveth you.* The next verse stresses the point further: *Therefore shall ye lay up these my words in your heart and in your soul, and bind them for a sign upon your hand, that they may be as frontlets between your eyes.*

The uniqueness of Torah study in Israel is reflected in the Jerusalem Talmud (*Nedarim* 6:8): "The Lord said: I prefer a small group in Israel to a large Sanhedrin outside of it."

Maimonides wrote in *Halachot Melachim* 8, *Halachot* 9–12, that it is forbidden to leave Israel for another country unless it is for the purpose of studying the Torah, marrying, or saving somebody from the pagans, and then one must return to Israel. To reside abroad is forbidden, unless there is a severe hunger in Israel. The rule is to live in Israel even if the actual place is filled with pagans rather than to live abroad even in a mostly Jewish town.

He who leaves Israel gives up his connection with his source of life, and this is the reason why the leaders who left Israel were doomed. A Jew must make the effort to live in Israel. Those who left may have felt guilty.

Another observation of Maimonides is that Israel is a heritage and that that legacy is its strength. It is given from one generation to another eternally.

Notwithstanding his writings, Maimonides came to find that because of its impoverishment, the Land of Israel did not give him enough of an intellectual environment for him to continue his studies, and he left. Although this action may seem contradictory, his last wish was to be returned to the Holy Land, and he was buried in Tiberias.

In the sayings of Hazal (an acronym that stands for the Hebrew phrase meaning "Our Sages of Blessed Memory") in the Talmud and Midrashim, there are clear views about the obligation to make *aliyah* to Israel.

In the *Ketubot* tractate (110b), it is said, "Everybody is ascended to Israel," and Rashi explains: "a man must force all his family members to come with him to Israel and settle with him in Jerusalem." It is also forbidden to leave Israel for good. In a case where the wife wants to leave and her husband doesn't, she is forced to stay.

Maimonides even goes further, saying that if a slave intends to come and live in Israel, his owner is forced to come with him. If the owner wishes to leave Israel and go abroad, he cannot take his Jewish slave unless the latter agrees to go with him.

Ramban (Nachmanides) maintains that the mitzvah of settling in the Land of Israel is as important as any of the traditional 613 biblical commandments or precepts (*Taryag Mitzvot*) and is eternally valid.

The *Taryag Mitzvot* were first discussed by Rabbi Simlai, who was a second-generation *amora*. He was born in Nehardea in Babylonia but spent most of his life in the Land of Israel, in Lod and in the Galilee, and was a colleague of the grandson and great-grandson of Rabbi Judah Ha-Nasi. His *halakhic* rulings were known in Nezivin in Babylonia and in Antiochia in Syria; they dealt mainly with the intercalation of the month and the importance of charity. However, his most famous sermon was on the *Makot* tractate (23b) regarding the 613 commandments that were given to Moses. These consisted of 365 prohibitions ("do not"), corresponding to the number of days in the solar year, and 248 mandates ("do"), corresponding to the number of bones and important organs in the human body. Rav Simlai said of the mandates that each part of the human body would say: Do this mitzvah for me.

Thanks to Rav Simlai, the *Minyan Mitzvoth* literature (counting the mitzvahs) developed and was later expanded by Rav Saadyah Gaon and Maimonides, among others. The significance of the total of 613 comes from taking the numerical value of the word "Torah" in gematria—a system of assigning numbers to letters, whole words or phrases and finding numerical links—which is 611, and adding the first two commandments that were heard by the people of Israel directly from God (Exodus 20) rather than through Moses.

> 2: *I am the Lord thy God, which have brought thee out of the land of Egypt, out of the house of bondage.*

> 3: *Thou shalt have no other gods before me.*

Rav Saadyah ben Joseph (Saadyah Gaon), who among his many literary contributions wrote the book *Taryag Mitzvot*, was the central Jewish figure during the period of the *geonim* (heads of the Babylonian yeshivas). Known as the father of rabbinical literature for his huge linguistic output, he was considered the first Hebrew grammarian (Avraham Ibn Ezra crowned him *Rosh Zikney Leshon Hakodesh*, head of the holy language elders). He excelled in liturgical poetry known as *piyyut* (plural: *piyyutim*) and was responsible for the compilation and arrangement of his famous *Siddur* (Prayerbook).

He was also known as the philosopher who wrote *Emunot ve-De'ot* (*Beliefs and Opinions*), the first composition of medieval Jewry, which marks the opening of the history of the Jewish philosophy in that period. His influence on the Jewish medieval thought was great because of his authority as a great *halakhic* law-maker. He is also known for challenging the Karaite sect, which rejected the Oral Law, and for writing essays condemning them.

Saadyah was born in 882 CE in the Fium region in Egypt and died in 942 in Baghdad. From Egypt he went to the Land of Israel and later to Haleb and Baghdad. He was called up to head the Sura Yeshiva in Babylonia, and under his leadership it returned to its days of glory as a counterbalance to the Pumbedita Yeshiva.

According to an account given by the scholar Nathan HaBavli, Rav Saadyah was involved in a dispute with the *Rosh Hagola* or exilarch, David ben-Zakai, because he refused to ratify a will that would have benefited the exilarch greatly. Saadyah also opposed the head of the Pumbedita Yeshiva, Rabbi Cohen Zedek. Against this background he was banished by David ben-Zakai and removed from office. Rav Saadyah Gaon on his part banished the Rosh Hagola and appointed in his place the latter's brother, Yoshiyahu. Saadyah's critics were joined by Aharon ben Yoseph Serjada, one of Babylonia's wealthy Jews, who was close to the heads of Pumbedita Yeshiva and who published a booklet of insults against Rav Saadyah. Eventually Saadyah was forced to retire and give up his office as *gaon*, head of the yeshiva. Later on these two reconciled, and Saadyah returned to his chair as the head of Sura Yeshiva.

In *Taryag Mitzvot*, Saadyah included the mitzvah of settling in Israel. In his doctrine on ethics and the religious leadership, he claimed that in the worship of God there is a need for a wise law-maker who will make rules for a wise man to obey. *Taryag Mitzvot* was republished in 1897 in Paris (by I. Miller) and later on in Warsaw with a comprehensive annotation by Rabbi Y. P. Pirla. Despite being one of the chief sages of Babylonia, Saadyah Gaon was not afraid to interpret the Mishnah differently than did the Babylonian Talmud. He was influenced by formulations and interpretations of the Jerusalem Talmud, which he knew from his earlier life in Egypt and in the Land of Israel, and this experience may be the reason for his proud insistence on the principle of *Yishuv Eretz Israel* (settling in the Holy Land).

He was also courageous in not accepting some of the Babylonian rules of *halakhah*. Just as he would not have seen eye to eye with the Rambam (Maimonides) concerning the commandment to live in the Holy Land, he would also have disputed with "The Great Eagle" (an epithet for Maimonides) on Jerusalem's responsibility for the sanctification of the month. Sages such as Maimonides and Rav Hai Gaon thought that Saadyah just liked to debate issues, but the truth is that he evaluated, acted, and made his determinations according to how he thought it would be done in the Land of Israel, which for him was the important point. Maimonides also took issue with Saadyah's writings with regard to philosophy—Maimonides being guided by Aristotelian doctrines and Saadyah being partial to the (Moslem) Kalam. Ultimately, the former's prevalent influence in the thirteenth and fourteenth centuries brushed Saadyah's opinions aside.

THE HISTORICAL RIVALRY BETWEEN
BABYLONIA AND ISRAEL

Given the biblical imperative to live in the Land of Israel, the relationship between Israel and the Diaspora was problematic given the sacredness of Israel and the profaneness of the rest of the world. The sacredness of the Land of Israel was an ancient principle and the entire religious rite would be impossible without it. The People of Israel inherited the land by a decree of God, and so it was sacred and thus all the neighboring and hostile countries were considered profane soil during the Prophets' time. The Prophet Amos (7:17) warned: "And they shall die in a polluted land and Israel shall surely go into captivity forth of his land." Defining the Gentile countries as profane was meant to lock the gates of the Land of Israel in order to stop migration to other countries, and to inspire fear and guilt among those who considered leaving.

A question that occupies the scholars has to do with the Divine Presence in the Babylonian Exile. The term *Shechina be-Galuta*, "the Divine Presence in Exile," involves sadness and anticipation of the Messianic arrival. However, another statement by a Babylonian *amora* in the Midrash (interpretation) *Vayikra Rabbah*, which says *Gola le-Bavel ve-galta Shechina Ima*, "Exiled to Babylonia, and the Divine Presence is exiled there as well," wishes to provide some solace to the exiled. In the Babylonian Talmud Rabbi Yochanan states: "The Lord said: I shall not come unto Celestial Jerusalem until I come to Terrestrial Jerusalem" (*Taanit 5a*). Here the emphasis is on the salvation of Jerusalem and its reconstruction. In *Midrash Tanaim*, it is even graver: "The Divine Presence rests only upon he who was born in Israel and therefore it rested only on Benjamin, who was born in Israel, since all his brothers [the eleven other tribes] were born abroad."

This belief in the strength and holiness of the country was preserved in the spiritual center of Yavneh, which nurtured the continuous clandestine rebellion against the Romans and eventually brought on the heroic Bar Kokhba rebellion. The Romans mobilized legions from Gaul, Britain, and Germania, and even though they sustained heavy losses, they crushed the rebellion, massacring the Jews. In addition, the Roman emperor Hadrian set fire to more than half of the land. This catastrophe thinned out the number of Jews in the country and forced them into other lands. Each decree of punishment drove more Jews into exile in Babylonia. With time, the hardships of the remaining Jews in Israel only deepened the contention between the two spiritual centers.

It's unclear what share Babylonia has in the responsibility for the degradation of Israel at the time. Its rights in the scriptural domain are established and convincing, yet its "sins" are as well, and who but its three greatest scholars who left Babylonia to settle in Israel—Rabbi Elazar, Rabbi Ami, and Rabbi Yirmiyah—could testify for it. Rabbi Elazar quotes the furious prophecy of Hosea (13:14 ff.) as the reason for the exile to Babylonia. Rabbi Ami, who inherited Rabbi Elazar's chair at the yeshiva in Tiberias, worded an extremely sharp statement prohibiting Jews from obtaining any benefit whatsoever from living in Babylonia (noted in the Introduction to this volume).

However, all the warnings and denunciations did not stop Israeli inhabitants from leaving their homeland and immigrating to Babylonia. Yirmiyah warned that more and more people were leaving Israel to go to Babylonia and fewer and fewer were seen to be coming back.

The exile (*golah*) created a competitive state of affairs between the Israeli Jewry and the Babylonian Jewry. According to M. A. Tenenblat, in *Prakim Hadashim le-Toldot Eretz Israel u Bavel Bitkufat Hatalmud,* "New Chapters in the History of Eretz Israel and Babylonia in the Talmud Compilation Era" (Tel Aviv: Devir, 1966), a historical wrangle between Babylonia and the Land of Israel existed throughout the generations, and an emotional wrangle it was too. It was based on feelings of resentment and contempt that had begun in the days of the Return to Zion (*Shivat Zion*), when in 538 BCE the Persian King Cyrus declared that those who had been forced into Babylonian exile were not only permitted but encouraged to return to their countries of origin. However, many preferred the good life in Babylonia and chose to remain on their "pots of meat" (Exodus 16:3).

The Babylonian Jews saw those who elected to return to Israel as a combination of unworthy and inferior people. The snobbishness was not one-sided. Israeli Jews regarded some of the Jewish Babylonian immigrants returning to Israel as a combination of "imperfect" Jews, disqualified for marriage. Rabbi Elazar, the great Babylonian *amora* who settled in Israel at the time of Rabbi Yochanan, stated: "Ezra brought with him to Israel all the disqualified Jews, thus leaving Babylon as pure semolina," a place for an elite society.

The hardship of the Jews in Israel compared with the prosperity of the Jews in Babylonia was always an issue of tension between the two spiritual centers, especially when the Babylonian center rapidly outpaced that of Israel, with growing numbers of students and yeshivas, which spread throughout the country and generated a literary rivalry. Family ties were slackened and *aliyah* was replaced by migration. Eventually Babylonia took over the spiritual and emotional sovereignty of Israel. Israel had lost its attraction.

There are several references to this controversy in the Babylonian Talmud. In a debate on an alleged side issue, Rabbi Ami in Israel comments on the pretty dress of the Babylonian scholars as a proof that they are not true Torah learners. Against him Rav Yoseph, the typical arrogant Babylonian, praises the Babylonian scholars who "wear fringes and flowers to honor the Torah." Rabbi Yochanan rebukes Rabbi Ami for his words and explains that the Babylonian scholars are indeed Torah scholars and their ornate clothes only disguise the fact that they are exiles in a foreign land. However, Rav Joseph, the Babylonian, rejects this compromise and interprets the verse from Isaiah (27:6), referred to in the Introduction, as: "Jacob will take root in Babylonia; Israel shall blossom and bud in Babylonia; and fill the face of the world with fruit from Babylonia."

The argument divided the Babylonian scholars into two camps, those who immigrated to Israel, perhaps out of guilt for having earlier abandoned the Holy Land, and those who remained in Babylonia, snubbing the former. Sometimes the division boiled openly and was debated; at other times, it simply simmered under the surface.

Was the Babylonian Exile—the historic process that determined the fate of the Jewish nation and its homeland for 1,500 years—inevitable? And is there an element of determinism in the history of nations? Rabbi Akiva's philosophic rule "Everything is anticipated and the permission is given" is applied throughout the history of the Jews and allows us to gauge the responsibility of Jews in Babylonia for that period in general and toward the Land of Israel in particular.

After the death of Rabbi (Rabbi Judah Ha-Nasi, codifier of the Mishnah), not much changed in Israel. Rabbi's successors knew how to fare, internally and externally, with the "Evil Kingdom," the Roman ruler. Whether out of resignation following the bloodshed of Bar Kokhba's suppressed rebellion or out of gratitude for the gift of the Mishnah that they inherited from Rabbi, they knew how to dull the prohibitions and decrees of punishment, to get along. There is a tradition of Hieronimus, who said that the Jews themselves saw in the rule of Severus Septimus and Caracala after him a kind of a fulfillment of Daniel's vision (Daniel, 11:34), which predicted the fall of the Jews but also indicated that they would receive a little help.

We may assume that when Rabbi transferred the presidency of the Sanhedrin to Raban Gamliel III, his son and successor, he must have taught him the art of its maintenance and this information was conveyed further down the line.

Jewish autonomy in Israel was actually never formally defined by the Romans; almost everything was dependent on the behavior of the Jews and their leaders, and on the attitude of the Romans, who, out of respect for the leadership of Rabbi and his house, turned a blind eye on the Jews for the most part. The Jewish president, head of the Sanhedrin, was considered as the premier personality and, apart from tax collection and trials of capital sins, he had full authority over the Jewish community. Rabbi's son, Raban Gamliel III, published a strict proclamation: "Be careful with the authorities; they bring a man closer only for their own benefit." This is a much lighter proscription than that of Shma'aya (in *Avot*, 1, 10), who at the time of Pompeius warned: "Don't make yourself known to the authorities."

This state of affairs lasted until the generation of Rabbi Yehuda Nesiya, Rabbi's grandson and also a president of the Sanhedrin, and indeed this period excelled in much spiritual activity. In these two generations, all the large and complex literature that was not included by Rabbi in the Mishnah— *baraitot, tosaftot, mechiltot,* and *midrashey halakhah*—were compiled and arranged by scholars like Rabbi Hiyya and his son Hizkiya.

· 4 ·

THE BUDDING GREATNESS OF THE
BABYLONIAN EXILE

*I*T'S NOT KNOWN for sure whether the greatness of Jewish Babylonia is due to the great deeds of Rav and Shmuel alone or whether there already were concealed seeds in the soil of this Jewry that sprouted under the influence of these two great men. These two did not arrive in Babylonia to a completely desolate country; in Nehardea and Nehar Pakod there were Torah centers during the *tannaim* period, but Sura and the southern villages were devoid of places to study.

Shmuel was a very clever expert jurist and also an erudite scholar both in the Torah and its literature as well as in contemporary science. Rav, on the other hand, was a very creative scholar. And if it was said that "everywhere *halakhah* is like Rabbi Yochanan's," it is because Yochanan, who was younger than Rav and Shmuel, was unique in his knowledge of the *halakhah* and the *aggadah*, and his sharpness was spiced by midrashic poetry and *Melitza* (fine phraseology, usually biblical), all well rooted in the beloved reality of Israel.

Rav's greatness was also spiced with the Israeli scent. He arrived in Babylonia while Rabbi was still alive in Israel. At the time, Israel was much respected by the Babylonian Jews. Even so, at first they didn't accept Rav's authority as easily as he might have expected. They considered him Babylonian like them. That he had studied in Israel was not reason enough to gain their respect. However, in time he won them over.

Up until Rabbi's tenure of office as president of the Sanhedrin in Israel, and prior to the beginning of Rav and Shmuel's activity in Jewish Babylonia, there were three large Torah study centers already in existence in Babylonia: Nehardea, Nezivin, and Hutzel, which geographically were close to Israel. All of their teachers had studied in academies and schools in Israel, which had dominance over all exile communities, of which Babylonia was the largest and most important. Most of these teachers truly loved the Holy Land and, despite the bad times, were attracted to it and went there to study and to settle as a first fulfillment of their duty to obey the commandments. In particular during Rabbi's life, many outstanding scholars from Babylonia filled the yeshivas of Tiberias, Bet She'arim and Zippori, a fact that more than once caused envy and malice because these "new *olim*"(those who make *aliyah*) gathered together in their "Babylonian" synagogues in Israel and didn't mingle with the native pupils.

At the time, Rabbi and the scholars close to him were busy sifting the abundant material for the codification of the Mishnah. His huge creation was accepted in the Diaspora with enthusiasm and pride and was considered to be as eternal as the Holy Scriptures.

Of course there was no shortage of bitterness and friction in a society that suffered from economic hardships. However, in a spiritually active atmosphere, even human weakness and differences fade from view, and poor and rich Babylonians and local scholars were considered equal. Rabbi chose as his assistant a Babylonian *tanna*, Rabbi Yitzhak bar Avdimi, who was also called Ruba, with whom he reviewed the entire Mishnah until its final completion.

Rabbi's leadership and the Jewish sovereignty over a fragmentary Israel, if it could be considered as such, focused only in the spiritual, religious, and social domains, with the political and civil authority under the constant supervision of the Roman rule. After Rabbi's death a controversy between the two spiritual centers—Israel and Babylonia— broke out regarding ultimate control over the academies, schools, and rabbinical courts (the *Yeshiva*, the *Bet Midrash*, and the *Bet Din*). This controversy surely undermined the supremacy of Israel over Babylonia. As a result of the controversy, many great scholars left Israel for Babylonia and many fewer scholars came to Israel.

Rav was one of those who left Israel for good and settled in Babylonia. His and Shmuel's achievements laid the groundwork for the Babylonian spiritual centrality to take over from Israel's. Both Rav and Shmuel, separately, were prepared and instructed for their future roles in Babylonia, Shmuel by his father Abba bar Abba Hacohen (*Abu'ha di*

Shmuel), and Rav by his uncle Rabbi Hiyya.

The reason Shmuel left Israel and returned to Babylonia is thought to have centered on the fact that he was not granted an ordination (*semikhah*) from Rabbi. Suffering from ill health in his late years, Rabbi decreased the number of his *smichot,* citing his total occupation in the arrangement of the Mishnah and in his roles with study centers and other positions. But there were other reasons as well.

Rabbi was intolerant of criticism or even objection. Once, while at a dinner in Rabbi's home, junior pupils of Rav's uncle Rabbi Hiyya who were a bit tipsy cursed him and the presidency by saying that the Messiah would not come until this institution came to its end. Such incidents, which exposed the concealed animosity, must have chilled Rabbi's attitude and emotions towards the Babylonians and increased his mistrust in them.

The chief goal of the presidency of those days was to fortify the remains of the Jewry in Israel. This could have been achieved, among other ways, through the constant immigration to Israel of wealthy Babylonian Jews and their sons, who would study in the local yeshivas and, it was hoped, would remain in the country. However, if the Israeli scholars carried even a faint suspicion that the true intention of the new arrivals was to return to Babylonia, they were cautious about ordaining. This mistrust was further increased by the fear that a concentration of ordained scholars in Babylonia might undermine or even destroy the *halakhic* centrality of Israel and, as a result, its presidential institution.

As we saw, this fear was expressed two generations later by Resh Lakish, brother-in-law and friend of Rabbi Yochanan, who told Rabbah bar bar Hana, one of the *nachoti* (the messengers who went between Israel and Babylonia), "God, I hate [all of] you," because they preferred to live in Babylonia.

In reality, Shmuel probably did not get a *semikhah* in Israel because his ancestry was unclear. It was suspected that his mother had been raped while his father was away on his trading business, although there were attempts to deny this and to explain his conception in some miraculous way. Since Shmuel was in his thirties and a physician as well, it is understandable that he preferred to return to Babylonia. In any case, Israel at that time was a lesser place for Shmuel's scope. His father was a wealthy leader with deep roots in Babylonia and must have brought up his son along the same lines. There his cleverness and skills were recognized, and clearly he didn't need a *semikhah* or any rabbinical title or recommendation whatsoever.

Shmuel's fruitful activity, both spiritual and social, left its impact on many generations after him and remained forever within the Babylonian Talmud, no less than Rabbi Yochanan's impact in Israel. He was a sharp and deep genial scholar as well as being honest and friendly with his pupils. In his yeshiva in Nehardea, he educated hundreds of pupils who also went to Sura to study with Rav, and many of them eventually immigrated to Israel to sit before Rabbi Yochanan and Resh Lakish.

However, the so-called Babylonian vanity did not escape him altogether. He tended to patronize Rabbi Yochanan, the spiritual giant of Israel in both *halakhah* and *aggadah*, even though the rulings of the "father of the Jerusalem Talmud" always prevailed over that of Rav and Shmuel.

Once Rabbi Yochanan wrote to Shmuel, addressing him as "Our Friend in Babylonia." Shmuel was offended and reacted by sending back a calendar he had made for the intercalation of the next sixty years, just to prove his skills. On the other hand, Rabbi Yochanan did express respect for Rav, whom he addressed as *Rabenu* (our Master).

Shmuel was the first to shift the spiritual center of gravity from Israel to Babylonia. He established a large competing academy in Nehardea, before that of Rav in Sura. Researchers think that the Nehardea Yeshiva was more Israel-loving than Sura's, and Sura's was more so than Pumbedita, but this pattern was not a fixed one for the future. Each subsequent head of these yeshivas would act differently. What all of them did equally was to amplify and increase the Torah instruction in Babylonia relative to the size of its local Jewish community. And perhaps while busying themselves with this goal, they ignored the crisis developing in Israel under the Roman thumb that encouraged its desertion. And as in a vicious circle, the Babylonian Jewry felt it their duty to cultivate the existence of this large Jewish expansion as the substitute and heir to the gradually sinking Israel. It may be that they regarded it as necessary from Shmuel's time onward, whether knowingly or unknowingly, to free their neck from the spiritual yoke of the Israeli leadership.

Out of the Babylonian vanity, which increased along with their spiritual swelling, and with the codification of the Babylonian Talmud, the Babylonian scholars gained possession of the lineage of the spiritual leadership. This lineage, which was entirely Babylonian, was eternalized in a Talmudic assertion, *de'amar Mar,* which means stated by either Rav or Shmuel: When Rabbi Akiva died, Rabbi (Judah Ha-Nasi) was born. When Rabbi died, Rav Yehuda was born. When Rav Yehuda died, Rabbah was born. When Rabbah died,

Rav Ashi was born … as was said: *Ve-zarach hashemesh u'va hashemesh,* "the sun rises and the sun sets." (*Kiddushin* 72b, and its parallels in *midrashim*).

De'amar Mar indicates that with the death of Rabbi in Israel, the entire spiritual heritage moved to Babylonia. From then on there was no recognition of Israeli sages (although in the Babylonian Talmud there isn't a single issue without Rabbi Yochanan's participation and most of the time with his final ruling). They left out the generations of Israeli scholars who wrote and arranged the Jerusalem Talmud and granted to the Babylonian Talmud that vigor and juice, that scent and flavor of the air and atmosphere of Israel, without which the Babylonian Talmud might not have become the faithful inheritor of the national creation.

Clearly it was not Shmuel, nor Rav, in person who determined this statement of lineage, which continues past their deaths; however Shmuel was the first to cut off Babylonia's affiliation with Israel by preparing Babylonia for this mission, as if the nation and its cultural center in Israel were already on the verge of annihilation. This was such an accepted fact that the editor of the Babylonian Talmud could put the above statement in the mouth of *Mar* (an Aramaic term of respect, roughly translated as "lord" and probably referring here to Shmuel).

True, Shmuel, the genial scholar, was wholly Babylonian, since he lived and died in the Babylonian Exile. However, we can assume that the Israeli scholars regretted the fact that he did not come to live in Israel, at the very least to be buried there, rather than in the "impure country," as the Israeli scholars referred to the *amoraim* graves following the statement of Rabbi Elazar (*Ketubot* 111a), who was Shmuel's pupil in Babylonia and who was considered even greater when he eventually settled in Israel next to Rabbi Yochanan and Resh Lakish.

Shmuel was adored by the entire Babylonian Jewry for his wisdom and activity on their behalf. His denomination *Mar* indicates the love and respect accorded him even by Israelis, who cherished his logic and sharpness of mind. In the Jerusalem Talmud he was often called Rabbi Shmuel, though everybody knew that he never received a rabbinical *semikhah*. Eventually he and Rav were called by the Jerusalem Talmud *Raboteynu she'be'Bavel*, "our Rabbis-Masters in Babylonia."

One wonders if Shmuel was genuinely beloved in Israel, since every informed person there saw that Shmuel devoted his intellect and gifts to Jewish Babylonia, thus contributing, perhaps unintentionally, to the distancing of Babylonia from its legacy and its expropriation of the spiritual, religious, and ethical reign of Israel. And one wonders if Shmuel felt any guilt at wresting these powers away from the Holy Land, since until Shmuel's days, Israel was the only religious ruler of the entire Jewish nation.

RAV ESTABLISHES A SPIRITUAL CENTER OUTSIDE ISRAEL

Shmuel, with all his greatness, could not have gained his achievements without the help of Abba Arikha who, as we saw in Chapter 2, became known by the short and modest name of Rav.

Rav realized that he could not inhabit the same Torah study center as Shmuel, and he established the historical yeshiva of Sura, when he was already middle-aged. Rav had studied first in Israel, where his uncle, Rabbi Hiyya, had taken him. At least twice during that time he returned to Babylonia, where he stayed for a period of time, once to get married, before returning to Israel. His second and longer visit to Babylonia may have been due to the death of his parents, but he also may have been investigating opportunities to settle there. He understood that he had no chance of attaining public respect for his spiritual status in Israel under Rabbi's presidency. He returned to Israel for a short time only after the death of Rabbi, in order to try to obtain a "full *semikhah*" from Rabbi's sons. A portion of the *semikhah* given to him by Rabbi was missing, the part of *Hatarat Bechorot*, which was the authority to cancel the obligation to give the firstborn animal meat to the priests. Rav petitioned for the missing portion, but Rabbi's son, Rabban Gamliel, would not grant it. Disappointed, Rav packed his belongings and left Israel, this time for good.

Rav must have thought it for the better, since the living conditions in Babylonia were far superior to those in Israel, where more and more regulations were necessary to mitigate the hardships, to encourage *aliyah*, and to prevent the immigration to Babylonia. Also Israel lacked the spiritual space of Babylonia. Everything in Israel was concentrated around the president and his ruling area, that is, the Tiberias–Bet She'arim–Zippori triangle with the addition of small "bays" mingled with foreign populations like Lod in the south and Keysarin in the west.

Rabbi was managing his affairs with "a high hand," thus suppressing any objection. No wonder, therefore, that Rav, the son of a privileged Babylonian family, was tempted to return home, where he would be more than welcome. Rabbi, by virtue of his role, kept watch over what was going on in Babylonia and chiefly over the Babylonian Jewry's attitude toward Israel, and he would question the scholars who visited Babylonia about any shift in public opinion there regarding their affiliation to the Holy Land, using his influence to try to prevent it.

All this was surely felt in Rabbi's house in Israel, further strengthening their suspicions of the ex-Babylonians, who, while willing to live in Israel, opted for Babylonia when they had an opportunity to choose between the two.

Rav was a prominent scholar who grew up, was educated, and became well known in Israel. His departure, at a more than ripe age, was a national tragedy. Although there is no hint in either Talmud of Rabbi's reaction to Rav's defection, one may assume that it was significant. At the same time, one may also assume that Rabbi felt it safer to let him go to Babylonia rather than remain in Israel, where Rav could impede the presidency and overshadow Rabbi's sons and heirs.

Some even think that Rav's greatness reduced the greatness of Israel, since he took everything from it and gave it nothing. But one can see his return to Babylonia as a positive step as well. Rav, with his depth, skills, and gifts, and of course his pupils, constructed the first layers of the Babylonian Talmud, the Talmud without which the Jewish nation would not have survived through the persecutions and calamities in its diverse exiles.

In Babylonia, Rav became a central figure, together with Shmuel. He was particularly known for his strictness regarding questions of prohibition and permission. Some scholars have wondered about his indifference toward the sovereignty of Israel after he settled in Babylonia. Sources concerning this issue are scarce; however there is one story that provides a rather interesting illustration. Rav had a conflict with the Israeli presidency, and even with his colleague and friend Shmuel, over granting permission in the Holy Land to use oil produced by Gentiles. Jewish oil could be brought only from the Temple Mount, a place that was extremely dangerous to get to in those days. The presidency therefore allowed the use of oil from Gentiles. Rav, however, insisted on prohibiting its use, but he was forced to retract his objection by Shmuel, who threatened to declare him a *Zaken Mamre*, "a rebellious old man," if he persisted in his refusal.

During the last *tannaim* period and the first generations of the *amoraim*, it was strictly prohibited to leave Israel. In the Tosefta (77, 65) it is said, "He who leaves the country in time of peace and goes abroad, is as if he is an idolater." This was a fixed *halakhah*. And Rabbi Hanina bar Hama said of an emigrant that "he who abandons his mother's bosom equals he who embraces a foreign bosom." In this matter we should point out that Rabbi saw the need to relax this *halakhah*, since he himself used to send messengers to Babylonia to convey some of the Israeli study, encourage *aliyah*, and request material assistance.

After Rabbi's death and the impoverishment of his inheritance, Israel stopped being economically independent. It needed urgent and constant help from the Diaspora, and first of all from neighboring Babylonia. The decrees and prohibitions caused its inhabitants to flee from their homes in both towns and villages to wherever possible. It was getting more and more difficult to make a living. In contrast, the *amoraim* in Babylonia became richer. Rav, who had arrived in Babylonia empty-handed and in his first years there lived poorly, eventually gained wealth and bought property, houses, and fields. The same was true of Rav Huna, Rav Yehuda, Abbaye, Rav Papa, Rav Ashi, and his son. All of them were wealthy. These *amoraim*, as well as other leaders, including the heads of the exiled community, the exilarchs, ignored the calamities and hardships taking place in Israel as much as they could, and indeed the contacts between the two centers gradually declined. However, the Babylonian Jewry could not renounce Israel completely while they were still obliged by its spiritual rule. So what did they do? To free themselves from the Israeli yoke, they built synagogues, symbolic replacements for the Temple in the Holy Land.

Rav and his inheritors set the cornerstone for the huge structure of the Babylonian Talmud. He could have done the same in Israel with Rabbi Hanina bar Hama and Rabbi Yochanan, but perhaps it was Providence that guided him back to Babylonia and to his creation there when the Divine Presence deserted Israel and the remains of the nation resembled a dried-up tree. Be that as it may, the Babylonian scholars admitted their guilt and acknowledged their sin toward Israel. This action is evident in the Babylonian Talmud, which contains many bitter statements about these Babylonian scholars made by the Israeli scholars.

What was the reason for the manifest hostility between Israel and Jewish Babylonia? Why the dozens of observations, especially in the Jerusalem Talmud but also in some midrashim of Rabbi Yochanan and his friends and pupils, expressing scorn and mockery toward the Babylonian scholars? The probable answer is the threat of ceding Israel's authority to a Babylonian spiritual independence.

The Babylonian Jews traced their distinguished lineage back to the House of David and matched it against the low status of the Israelis. The Israelis, of course, rejected this arrogant claim and would never agree to Babylonia's replacing them in importance. Resh Lakish's statement in the Jerusalem Talmud says it very clearly: "If someone will tell me that there is a history in Babylonia [hinting to their boasting about their distinguished lineage], I shall go and get him myself; and now, all our teachers and scholars together will not be able to find him [because he is nonexistent]."

This statement by Resh Lakish was answered in the name of Rav, regretting the Israeli repudiation of the Babylonian distinction and affirming that even were this distinction to be taken from them, they were still preferable to all other exiles.

Rabbi Yochanan went on to wonder: Are there old people in Babylonia, since the Torah promises longevity only on the soil of the Holy Land?

Resentment against Jewish Babylonia never really slackened, and in later generations the scholars of Israel did their utmost to cause the Babylonian Jews to acknowledge their guilt, and tried to make them understand that the Babylonians held the key to the existence of the remaining Jewry in Israel. Sadly, after Rabbi Yochanan's death, no other leader came forward who had his great wisdom and influence in this complex area between Israel and Babylonia, and as a result their relations were never repaired.

· 5 ·

THE GOOD LIFE OF THE EXILARCHS
AND THE *AMORAIM*

*W*ITH THE CONTINUED strengthening of the Babylonian Jewry, which had already been strong before Rabbi's time, an attempt was made to sort out the question as to whether the authority and power of the exilarch, who was the leader of the Jews in Babylonia, extended to the Jewish population in the Land of Israel as well. There was a dialogue about it between Rabbi Hiyya, the Babylonian scholar who sat in Israel, and Rabbi, who was the Israeli president. A compromise of sorts was attained with Rabbi's silent consent. Since the number of Torah scholars in Babylonia was greater than that in Israel, it was decided that the exilarch would discipline and rule both the Babylonian Exile as well as Israel, until the return of the Kingdom of the House of David. Meanwhile in Israel the president would remain the spiritual leader and legislator and would determine the religious modes of life. This bona fide, but strange, compromise held on for two hundred years until the decline of the presidency and the final ruin of the Israeli Torah center.

There are contrary Talmudic statements, several versions of which appear in the *Horayot* tractate, where this illusionary fraternity between Jewish Babylonia and the spiritual and *halakhic* center in Israel is shattered. Jewish Babylonia was determined to achieve religious-spiritual sovereignty as well and not wait for Israeli rulings, leaving those in the Holy Land to deal only with the *halakhot* of prohibition and permission, which according to the Mishnah and the Tosefta were the monopoly of Israeli scholars.

And there is an *aggadic* (legendary) Babylonian story (in *Bava Kamma* 117a–b) in which Rav Kahana, Rav's pupil, argues with Rabbi Yochanan about some unexplained *halakhot,* and also in which the latter comes out defeated and ashamed. However, there is no response to this story anywhere in the Jerusalem Talmud by Rabbi Yochanan or Resh Lakish or their pupils. Therefore it may be a fictional story that was added later with an eye toward discrediting Yochanan.

A more positive reaction to the so-called "compromise" reached by Rabbi and Rabbi Hiyya is a statement from Rabbi Mana in the Jerusalem Talmud (in *Avodah Zarah*): "The world cannot contain less than 30 *Tzaddikim* (Righteous).... At times most of them are in Babylonia and a few of them in Israel, and at times most of them are in Israel and a few of them in Babylonia. *And the world is fine when most of them are in Israel.*"

The exilarchs, whose lineage could be traced back to the House of David, granting them celebrity and distinction, behaved as if they were royalty. They and the *halakhic* wise men also accumulated economic power and made themselves an elite group. There are stories in the rabbinic literature, both direct and inferred, about their extravagant lifestyle. This lifestyle actually closely resembled that of rulers in the Oriental countries in general but also of their counterparts in Israel—the presidents. Their great wealth stemmed from their immovable assets (land, houses), which gave them great power. A mention of this power is found in *Bava Batra* (36a), where the Gemara words are explained as: "and they [the exilarchs] are not afraid to protest since they will arbitrarily take whatever and whenever they wish." In *Bava Kamma* (102b), the figure of the exilarch is drawn as striking fear in everyone, since they were dependent on him. One of the Israeli scholars who came back from Babylonia described the conduct of the exilarch's household as "licentious" (*Jerusalem Megillah* 73; *Gittin* 7a).

The relationship between the exilarchs in Babylonia and the presidents in Israel was mainly formal, but then we know only about those whose memory was preserved. One of the formal issues was the intercalation of the calendar year. This was important for the unity of the People of Israel, to ensure the celebration of the Jewish holidays on identical dates in both Jewish centers. In that case, the Babylonian sages accepted the instructions given by the Israeli president.

The leadership positions of Israel and Babylonia were similar, both in their status in the community and in their dominance over the secular life, but some Babylonian leaders had special privileges.

When envoys from Israel arrived in Babylonia to collect money and refused to accept responsibility for the amounts collected, the local rabbinical court chastised them. The envoys were startled to see the religious judges wearing huge hats, actually as tall as their wearers, bearing names they were given by the Babylonian rule, and they were also daunted by the local swift judgment and punishing procedures, "a strap moving up and down," the Jerusalem Talmud wrote. According to the Babylonian Talmud, the judges also dealt with capital offenses: O*mrim harogu, horgin,* "They say: kill! And they kill." (*Gittin* 14b), meaning that they had full juridical authority to execute criminals, an extraordinary power.

Nevertheless, a connection existed between the two most important courts of justice of the time, the *Batey Din,* in Israel and in Babylonia. One story (*Sanhedrin* 31b) tells about an address from Israel to Mar Ukva, Rosh Hagola, regarding a legal case. (*Mar,* meaning "lord" in Aramaic, was a term of respect adopted by the families of the exilarch and later came to replace the title "Rav" in Babylonia.) The case involved a Jew appealing to the court in Tiberias about his brother Jeremiah, who, according to him, injured him (perhaps even castrated him) or cheated him in money matters. The court requested Mar Ukva to try the defendant in Babylonia, and if Jeremiah refused to obey the judges there, they should send him to the court in Tiberias to be tried.

The same Mar Ukva sent two personal letters to Rabbi Elazar in Tiberias begging his advice on how to respond to his opponents who threatened to give him away to the authorities.

However, there were no visits of Israeli presidents to Babylonia, just visits of scholars and, of course, of the messengers (the *nachoti*), either for keeping up the connections or for reasons of politeness.

A well-known *amora* visited Babylonia and stayed at the exilarch's home; the reason for this visit is unknown, but one of the interpreters thinks that he came to protest the extravagant lifestyle of his host and entourage, and therefore he may have been sent there by the Israeli president. As was mentioned, the exilarchs had many agricultural assets—wheat fields, fruit groves, and large herds—and therefore many slaves and servants. Some of these slaves were not careful with all the *halakhic* rules and commandments, a fact that caused criticism from various scholars over the years. The exilarchs would appear in public like kings, carried by slaves in a golden carriage and followed by dozens of people. The same was told about Rav Huna, who was only a member of the Rosh Hagola family but who drove around town in a golden carriage.

There are stories about the luxuriousness of their personal life as well as their use of Gentile customs. One exilarch was said to go to bed and get up in the morning singing. *Gittin* (7a) mentions the custom (taken from the Eastern court) of women slaves entertaining the ruler by dancing and singing, morning and evening. The banquets the exilarchs gave also displayed their wealth. One assumption about the source of their wealth is that they collected fixed taxes for the upkeep of their court. This is not certain, however. What *is* certain is that all their visitors, as was the custom in the Orient, would arrive with expensive presents. And their large estates, which they must have inherited, provided them with equally large incomes.

The exilarchs' strong economic status relieved them from dependence on the public opinion or approval of the scholars and rendered their rule almost absolute. Such was their exalted position that in the year 520, when there were no more presidents in Israel, exilarch Mar Zutra fled the Babylonian authorities, arrived in Tiberias, and was appointed head of the Sanhedrin, a great honor.

The Relations between the Scholars and the Exilarchs

The contacts between the exilarchs and the sages were conducted on various levels. Their aim was cooperation in the exilarch's court and leadership of the Jewish community, with joint appearances in public on such occasions as the High Holidays or public fasts. These contacts included courtesy visits by the scholars to pay their respects at the homes of the exilarchs, where the order of seating reflected the scholars' importance and a possible indication of future appointments.

The exilarchs would invite scholars, at times dozens of them, to dine with them on Friday nights and on holidays. The same was done by the presidents in Israel. The only difference between the two centers was that in the home of some of the Babylonian exilarchs, scholars would often admonish the house servants on their "licentiousness." There were cases in which scholars would scold the servants for disregarding rules for keeping the Sabbath. There are also tales citing servants' unprovoked cruelty and coarse behavior toward certain scholars, not to mention toward the simple folk. There is a story that Rav Amram Hasida was thrown by the exilarch's servants into the snow and then taken by the exilarch's wife to the burning hot ritual bath (*mikveh*). The explanation for this behavior, given by Rashi, was that the scholar must have aggravated them with his prohibitions, and probably not for the first time.

Another incident ended in the death of Rav Zavid, head of the Pumbedita Yeshiva. When he visited the home of the exilarch, he forbade them to eat a herring with burned or roasted egg. When other scholars were consulted, two permitted it and one—Rabbi Yochanan from Israel—forbade it. Rabbi Hiyya, an occasional visitor at the exilarch's home, ruled that two are stronger than one; therefore they should be obeyed. However, when Rav Zavid told them not to obey Rabbi Hiyya, the exilarch's people gave Rabbi Zavid a glass of vinegar to drink and that caused his death.

Such testy relations between the scholars and the exilarchs' people testify to the depraved atmosphere that prevailed in some of the exilarchs' homes during the *amoraim* period, a situation that did not exist in Israel. While there were foreign servants at the presidents' homes in Israel, their behavior was molded by their masters and never reached this level. These stories also highlight the courage of some of the scholars who dared to go against the corruption, negligence, or scorn on the part of the exilarchs and their household staff.

More proof of the autocratic rule of the exilarchs is seen in their power to grant privileges to some of the Babylonian *amoraim* in the commercial domain. It is thought that the Torah scholars in Babylonia were exempted from certain payments or work—like the construction of a wall around the town for defense purposes—that were required from all the others. In the case of the construction of the wall, their exemption demonstrates the self-esteem of the *amoraim*, who would boast of their unity with the Torah. In other words, the Torah defends Israel and the Torah learners defend Israel, and therefore it is beneath their dignity to go out to work together with the rest of the town's inhabitants. The defense costs were rather high, since many of the towns and settlements in Babylonia were located on the border and vulnerable to robbery by Arab nomadic tribes from the Great Syrian Desert. Their exemption from payment for the construction of the walls similarly proves their social status.

During the days of the *amoraim*, the wealth that was accumulated by the Babylonian leadership distanced them from the modest and simple life commanded by the Torah. The *amoraim* created an elitist group in Babylonia. They took care to maintain the existence of the Jewish people there and reinforce its inner strength against the redundant political situation of Israel since the end of the third century, and they stressed their responsibility regarding their future. Simultaneously they reinforced their own economic welfare, nesting their own homes, creating a cozy Jewish island where they felt safe and comfortable, away from their suffering homeland.

Along with the privileges they received, the Torah scholars demanded additional boons. The *Cohanim* (priests, descendants of Aaron, brother of Moses) among the Babylonian *amoraim* would receive presents similar to what was customary among the Cohanim in Israel. Every slaughterer and butcher was required to give them three parts—the stomach, the cheeks, and the arm—of each beast, both cattle and sheep. Even if the butcher himself was a Cohen, he was required to give these to another Cohen. Thus we see that the *amoraim* in Babylonia and in Israel granted themselves the same rights as the original Cohanim had, a process which began in Israel after the destruction of the Second Temple. At that point the status of the Cohanim weakened greatly, and the Torah scholars increased their share of teaching and leading the people and therefore were entitled to demand a certain reward for their spiritual service. However, it should be noted that some of the Babylonian *amoraim* did donate part of their income to poor scholars.

In addition to their right to receive gifts of meat, the *amoraim* of Babylonia would claim the best cuts when buying meat; this was a matter of prestige. The following story illustrates this custom: A man from Nehardea went to the slaughterhouse in Pumbedita to buy meat. When he placed his order, he was told to wait until the servant of Rav Yehuda Bar Yehezkiel came, and then they would serve them both. The man from Nehardea got angry and inquired: who is this Yehuda, son of a roast-eater, who gets in front of him? When Rav Yehuda was told what happened, he banished the man.

In Pumbedita, it was the custom to let the sages buy the best cuts of meat before the rest of the people, but it was not the custom in Nehardea. This privilege testifies to the senior social status of the *amoraim* in their own towns.

Another benefit for the Babylonian *amoraim* was the excellent unpaid or partly paid (it's not certain) hospitality they enjoyed in the landlords' homes, depending on their importance. There are stories that illustrate their relationship based on "barter." Some Torah scholars would lend legal advice to their hosts in return. The same was true in Israel. There were those, of course, who exploited the generosity of their hosts. Shmuel talked about certain scholars who did so, and it was frowned upon. There is an interesting statement by several Babylonian *amoraim*, among whom was Abbaye:

> *Every scholar who eats around will eventually destroy his home and widow his wife and orphan his fledglings, and forget his study, and will be disputed and unheard and will desecrate God's name and defame his mentor's and father's name and give himself and his sons and grandchildren till the end of all generations, a bad name.*

This statement was meant to deter the Torah scholars from overstaying their welcome in the homes of their hosts.

Historian Heinrich (Hirsch Zvi) Graetz noted that at the time of an Israeli rebellion against the Romans, Babylonia suffered from an ethical crisis. The wealthy and luxurious lifestyle the Babylonian scholars had created for themselves set them apart as a snobbish class that behaved like royalty and scorned the simple folk. "Their innocence and simplicity were replaced by pride and love of power. Rabbis would go out dressed in silk and carried in golden seats by their slaves. The Teachers rose above the people and were no more part of them; they dominated them." They also had special privileges to buy and to sell, and to be tried first in the courts. Graetz talks bitterly about Rava, who virtually reigned over the Mahoza region and who, despite his wisdom, behaved improperly by granting his brother special privileges.

However, the *amoraim*, according to Graetz, were not a social caste; they were a special subdivision selected on the basis of their intellectual ability. It is true that they had political as well as religious motives—they wanted to lead the people. This aspiration fixed their perception of influence and leadership over the Jews in Babylonia. Like every other group that wants to rule, they wished to be economically independent of the landowners and of the exilarch and his multiple household members who did not always strictly keep the *halakhic* rules.

After the heads of the yeshivas as well as some rabbinical judges and teachers rose in economic status, the *amoraim* began to display their rank in public in fashions that were current. Actually Graetz is too harsh with his judgment of the Babylonian *amoraim.* There is no proof that they detached themselves from the people. The long historical development of the relationship between them and the populace tells us that in the first generations, some of the scholars were more detached than the *amoraim,* and the fact that they rose on the economic scale derives greatly from the cooperation and will of the ordinary householders.

We can only assume that the privileges of the merchants among the Babylonian *amoraim* contributed to their wealth. They also may have aroused annoyance among the merchants, landowners, and simple folk, but they were not the only ones.

ECONOMIC MOBILITY

One of the most interesting phenomena about the economic status of the Babylonian *amoraim* is their mobility. We know that some of the eminent heads of yeshivas and rabbinical judges (*Dayanim*) were very poor when they were young, and barely made a living. After their appointment, they became wealthy, some of them extremely so. This material success was due to the support they got from the landlords, with whom they had a complex relationship.

This upward mobility is unique to the Jewish community in Babylonia, since the native Persian society at the time was divided into rigid classes, each having its own defined and fixed political and economic rights. Within the class itself, everyone knew his place, and the ability to advance from a lower class to a higher one was not only uncommon, but forbidden unless it was a case of exceptional talent.

The following stories are illustrative: One day Rav Hana bar Hanilai met Rav Huna, who was head of Sura Yeshiva after Rav's death; Rav Huna was carrying a spade on his shoulder. Rav Hana wanted to relieve Rav Huna of the burden but was told: "Take my spade only if you carry one in your own town. If you don't, I do not wish to be honored by your shame." Rav Huna was expressing the negative attitude that was common among the Torah scholars toward doing physical work in public. Rav Huna himself would irrigate fields and may have also been a shepherd. We know that once when he wanted to buy wine and did not have the money, he pawned his sash. Later on, however, he rose to the rank of head of a yeshiva and became a wealthy man, who owned fields and vineyards, traded in wine, and also donated generously to the needy.

Another story tells about his successor, Rav Hisda, who, when he was young, abstained from eating appetite-arousing vegetables, since he had no money. Instead he accustomed himself to eating very little. When eventually he grew wealthy, he was heard to say that he still did not eat vegetables, because he could now afford meat and fish.

On the other hand, Rabbah's economic condition was unfortunate. The Gemara compares their economic conditions as follows: "In Rav Hisda's home there are sixty weddings, while in Rabbah's home, sixty beareavments; in Rav Hisda's there is bread made of semolina flour [which was expensive], while in Rabbah's home, people don't even have corn bread."

When he was young, Abbaye, head of Pumbedita Yeshiva, used to irrigate the fields by night and at times went hungry and even suffered from a physical disorder caused by hunger. However, in time he accumulated assets and employed tenants and workers. The same was true of Rav Papa, who started life very modestly, eventually ending up as a very wealthy man.

These examples testify to the phenomenon of upward economic mobility among some of the sages in Babylonia; however, the same opportunities probably were not available to the ordinary people, according to a statement of Rav Papa in *Gittin* tractate (30b).

The Routes to Wealth

The sages found their way to a richer lifestyle through gifts given to them, and perhaps through their own initiatives in agriculture and trade. Rav Hisda and Rav Papa, for example, became wealthy from selling ale. Some of the poorer scholars grew wealthy by marrying the daughters of wealthy men, since the match was considered a good one for both parties.

Some *amoraim* became wealthy when their wealthy relatives made them heirs, since people commonly preferred to bequeath their legacy to Torah scholars. Rav Amram Hasida's mother is said to have left her money to her son the scholar, and not to his brother. This was the custom in Israel as well; it is based on the *halakhah* which says: "A neighbor and a Torah scholar—the scholar comes first. A relative and a Torah scholar—the scholar comes first" (*Ketubot* 80b).

It is interesting to note that, since the end of the Second Temple days, people would bequeath to scholars who were not even related to them. The Babylonian Talmud tells about a man whose sons misbehaved, so he bequeathed his assets to Yonathan Ben Uziel, who was one of Old Hillel's pupils (*Bava Batra* 133b–104a). Such acts confirm the great respect and appreciation people felt toward the Torah scholars. In *Shabbat* tractate (119a) there is a conversation that may explain this attitude:

> *Wealthy people in Israel, why do they become wealthy? Because they give tithe. And why in Babylonia? Because they respect the Torah [and its scholars]. And in the rest of the countries? Because they respect the Sabbath. And how do they respect the Torah? The same as they respect the Sabbath, [i.e., with things such as expensive food and beautiful dishes].*

This means that landowners invested in the Torah learners as they invested in amenities for the Sabbath. The same thing happened in Israel, where they supported the Cohanim by giving them 10 percent of their fruit crops. In *Yoma* tractate (22b), it is said that when a person is appointed to a public position he becomes wealthy, and this occurred both in Israel and in Babylonia, where it was the custom not only to support but also to enrich the head of a yeshiva if he was struggling economically.

However, one must not forget that we are talking not only rights or privileges. The heads of the yeshivas were also serving as judges in a rabbinical court. And the *dayanim* (judges) and teachers were obliged, unequivocally, not to take any fee for their judgments. In *Mishna Bechorot* (4, 6), it is said: "He who takes a fee for his trying—his trials are invalid." The judge must not be in any way dependent on landowners or other generous donors. *Mishlei* (Proverbs 29:4) says: "The king by judgment establisheth the land: but he that receiveth gifts overthroweth it." And Rav Nachman bar Cohen explains: "If a *dayan* resembles a king who needs nothing, he will 'build the land,' and if he resembles a Cohen who begs in barns, he will destroy it" (*Ketubot* 105b). But the fact is that this rule was not always strictly obeyed.

The heads of the yeshivas were economically independent and could strongly reject any benefit from a person who wished to be tried by them. This is one of the reasons for the *amoraim*'s eagerness to get land, and for their commercial activity and initiatives, since their economic independence not only granted them a sturdy social status but also enabled them to act as autonomous religious leaders without a need to "flatter" the landowners or concede to pressure from extremely difficult citizens.

It was expected that a lower-class farmer who hoped to be appointed head of a yeshiva would change for the better, but this "change" was possible only if he was "enriched," as told by Rabbi Abahu regarding Rabbi Abba of Akko (Acre). It was improbable that the Babylonian Jews would welcome a poor head of a yeshiva, since doing so ran counter to the beliefs of people of the region, apart from the Christians and some ascetic sects. Especially in the ancient world, no distinguished person—*dayanim* or heads of yeshivas—were poor or manual workers.

The elaborate economic activity of the well-known yeshiva heads, judges, and teachers was no different from that of their community members in Babylonia; however, theirs was conducted in a stricter manner than that of the ordinary people. One of the typical features of their economic businesses was maximal profit for a minimal amount of work. This way they found the most favorable solution to the religious conflict, which was the need for time and energy to devote to the Torah studies and public teaching versus the time needed to support their own personal livelihood. They were not hermits, but neither did they wish to appear as social equals. They behaved in the same way as their local Persian counterparts who were always sons of rich people in a place where one's social status and importance were measured according to the size and number of their assets. Thus they confirmed Solomon's words: "Now there was found in it a poor wise man, and he by his wisdom delivered the city; yet no man remembered that same poor man" (Ecclesiastes 9:16). And elsewhere in this book: "Wisdom is good with an inheritance; and by it there is profit to them that see the sun" (Eccl. 7:11).

Quite a few of the famous scholars such as Rabbi Simeon ben Shetach, Old Hillel, Rabbi Zadok, Rabbi Hanina ben Dosa, and others were owners of large estates as well as being international tradesmen. Both ways of living, the modest and the extravagant, contributed to the design of their religious and public leadership. Both types were economically independent and resembled the prophets who knew how to resist tyrants and personal interests. It should be noted that the Babylonian scholars resided among multiple ethnic groups that lived as feudal or semifeudal societies. Their eagerness for wealth to strengthen their leadership positions had a different social and political background than that of their equivalent in Israel, and perhaps this is the reason for their constant motivation to accumulate assets. According to recent research, all the efforts of the Babylonian *amoraim* to obtain capital and property were intended for the purpose of providing for their pupils and increasing their number, thus glorifying the Torah and the yeshiva they headed.

There is, however, another interesting point that shows the contrast between the wealthy lifestyle of Shmuel and that of other contemporary religious leaders. During the third century in Persia, in a place close to the Jewish center in the town of Mahoza, there was a spiritual leader by the name of Mani (216–276 CE, founder of Manichaeism) who preached strict abstinence. He demanded that his followers abstain from eating meat, drinking wine, and having sexual relations, as well as partaking of all the other joys of life, including accumulation of wealth. This school of thought was quite contradictory to the lifestyle of Shmuel, who thought it was compulsory to enjoy material life. The Babylonian leadership viewed poverty negatively, chiefly because it compromised independence. One preacher said— and everybody seems to remember it—that three things are hard for the body: a heart stroke is hard, an intestinal sickness is even harder, but the worst is destitution. Poverty is bad but dependence on others is worse.

AFFIRMATION OF LIFE

The *amoraim* loved life and enjoyed good food and drink. It seems that their proximity to farming and food production shaped their appetite for material satisfaction. Among other pleasures they indulged in was their bodily health care, which seemed like self-gratification. Rav and Shmuel supported this self-gratification and encouraged people to enjoy good food. Rav told his pupil Rav Huna: "If you have [good food] enjoy it because there is no pleasure in Hell and

Death does not loiter.... People resemble grass, they shine and wither."

Shmuel's attitude can be summed up in the saying *carpe diem,* "seize the day." Rashi interpreted it as: "If you have money to please yourself, don't wait for tomorrow, because you may die and miss this pleasure. The world (we are leaving) is here today and gone tomorrow." However, perhaps these statements were said only to their pupils and not to the public. The scholars used to instruct their pupils individually and according to their kind.

The Babylonian scholars definitely savored life more than their counterparts in Israel and this pleasure is expressed in the *Birkot Hane'henin,* a group of blessings thanking God for the capacity to enjoy one's senses.

· 6 ·

THE ISSUES DIVIDING THE
TORAH CENTERS

---

*A*FTER THE BAR KOKHBA rebellion, the outcome of which was catastrophic, writes Rabbi Binyamin Lau in *Chachamim* ("Wise Men"), most of the surviving Jews in Israel found their new place in the Galilee, others were sold into slavery and exiled, and some chose to leave the country, as was explained so well by Rav Sherira Gaon in his "Epistle" *Iggeret*: Because the Temple was destroyed, they went to Beytar, and when Beytar was destroyed, the sages were scattered all over.

Three centers abroad mentioned in this context were Rome, Netzivin, and *Gola* (Exile), which is probably Babylonia. In the *Halakhah Midrash* for the book of *Devarim*

(Deuteronomy) we find an illustration of this situation: Rabbi Yehuda ben Batira, Rabbi Matya ben Harash, Rabbi Eleh Moadey Hanina, Rabbi Yehoshua, and Rabbi Yonathan, who left the country for Paltum and remembered Israel, wept and tore their clothes and recited this sentence: *Virashtem ota viyeshavtem ba ushmartem la'asot et kol hahukim ha'ele,* saying "living in the Land of Israel is equivalent to all the mitzvot of the Torah." And yet they left. Did they experience guilt for having escaped while others still suffered in the Holy Land?

Babylonia absorbed the refugees from Israel who fled there following the failure of Bar Kokhba and the resulting Roman decrees of prohibition. Among the important Jewish religious scholars there were Rabbi Yehuda ben Batira and Rabbi Hanina, who created an autonomous system of independent Torah studies.

Rabbi Hanina, who was a judge in the court in Yavneh, was one of the great scholars of his generation; however, not all the scholars agreed with some of his actions, which were at odds with his wisdom.

Rabbi Hanina, who was a nephew of Rabbi Yehoshua, decided to sanctify the months and to intercalate the years on his own initiative, without considering Israeli authority. The Hebrew calendar required the insertion of leap days or weeks or even months to keep it in line with the seasons and also to ensure that important dates were observed at the correct time of year. Since doing this was the exclusive right of the Israeli scholars, Rabbi Hanina's action could have caused a divide within the nation; the holidays would have been celebrated in different months in different places.

Rabbi Judah Ha-Nasi, with his sharp mind, managed to break through this scheme. He sent two great scholars, Rabbi Yitzhak and Rabbi Nathan, to rebuke Rabbi Hanina. They made it clear to him that no one in exile is allowed to do the intercalation by himself and that it should be left to the spiritual leadership of Israel. They also threatened him, in an epistle they brought with them, that if he did not accept their ruling, he could begin to sacrifice in the desert (a pagan rite). This situation could have caused the absurd occurrence that instead of *Eleh Moa'dey HaShem,* "these are God's holidays," they would be written as *Eleh Mo'adey Hananya,* "these are Hanina's holidays," or instead of *Ki MiZion Tetze Torah,* "For out of Zion will go forth the law and the word of the Lord from Jerusalem" (Isaiah 2:3), it would be said *Ki miBavel Tetze Torah,* "For out of Babylonia ..." (which is ironical, not biblical).

Hanina objected, "But Rabbi Akiva, too, was intercalating the calendar outside Israel!" And the scholars replied that Rabbi Akiva was the greatest scholar and there were no others like him. Rabbi Hanina answered: "I too did not leave behind in Israel scholars of my level." And their rejoinder was: "The kids you left behind grew up and became goats [meaning that the junior scholars became senior scholars] and they sent us here to you, telling us that if you'll obey us—good; otherwise you'll be banished."

Hanina was not persuaded. He claimed that he was more learned in the Torah than those who remained in Israel, and to obtain support for this stand, he went to Rabbi Yehuda ben Batira, who lived in Netzivin. When the latter heard his claim, he mounted a horse and rode to every Jewish settlement he could reach to order them to disregard

Hanina and continue to keep the holidays according to the
Israeli Bet Din.

Another story about Rabbi Hanina appears in *Midrash
Raba, Kohelet* 1:24: he once went to Kfar Nachum, near Tiberias, where there was a sect of heretics. They cast a spell over
him and made him ride a donkey on the Sabbath. He went
to his favorite uncle, Rabbi Yehoshua, who gave him an
ointment and he recovered from the spell. His uncle also
told him, "Since the donkey of this evil heretic brayed on
you, you cannot stay in Israel anymore." So Rabbi Hanina
left Israel and went back to Babylonia, where he eventually
died peacefully.

While the story is told in an enigmatic language, its
message is clear. The strong-minded Rabbi Hanina went
to Kfar Nachum to argue with the heretics who believed
in the Messiah who was riding his donkey and bringing a
world in which every day is a Sabbath. However, Rabbi
Hanina's strong-mindedness did not save him. He became
entangled in the Messiah issue and he too was already "riding the donkey," heralding the coming of the World of
Sabbath. His wise uncle, Rabbi Yehoshua, advised him to
walk away from this sect of heretics and have nothing to
do with them, and for safety's sake told him to leave Israel
and go to Babylonia. However, even in Babylonia he was
not convinced that the salvation of Israel was annulled,
and he continued to believe that Israel had already spread
outside its borders and therefore he would be permitted to
intercalate the calendar there.

The end of the story is interpreted from its wording in
the *Berachot* (63b), that the two delegates from Israel were
ordered to tell to "our brothers in exile": "If you obey us,

good, and if not, then Achia (the exilarch or the head of the exile) should climb one of the mountains, build an altar there, and Hanina (who was a Levite) will play the violin and they will declare: 'We have no share in the God of Israel,' since Hanina was convinced that the salvation had already occurred." To which all the people present there began to cry and said: "God forbid it! We do have a share in the God of Israel."

Underlined in this story was the conclusion that there were dangerous heretics in Israel, but they had no influence in Babylonia. Nevertheless, the authority for intercalating the calendar, and by extension the parent authority of Judaism, was to remain in Israel—for the time being.

The power that began to form in Babylonia also reached into the issue of genealogical purity. In this matter the Babylonians were very particular not only to remain as "clean semolina," but also to declare that the best Jewry lived in Babylonia and in this respect they were above the Israeli Jewry.

Rabbi Hanina summed up the issue, saying all the countries constituted a dough to Israel, and Israel was a dough to Babylonia, meaning Israel is above all countries, but Babylonia is above Israel.

In *Kiddushin* (71a), it is said: In Rabbi's days (Judah Ha-Nasi) it was thought that the Babylonian Jews were less pure, unlike the Israeli Jews, since they were from mixed marriages, marriages between Jews and those who were "unqualified" (Gentile or half-Gentile). Ironically, Rabbi himself was a descendant of Hillel, a Babylonian who made *aliyah* to Israel.

During the tenure of Rav Huna, the first *Rosh Gola* (head of the Diaspora), a genuine soap opera took place between

him and Rabbi. Rav Huna had proclaimed that his family
tree reached back to the House of David, the same as Rabbi
himself. In addition, Rav Huna contended that his lineage
was closer to David, since it was traced through his father
while Rabbi's lineage was traced through his mother. (Rav
Huna was from the tribe of Judah, which was more important than the tribe of Benjamin, Rabbi Judah Ha-Nasi's
tribe). Rabbi very fairly declared that he would agree to step
down from the presidency and allow Rav Huna to take his
place, but only if Rav Huna returned to Israel. Rabbi didn't
think that Rav Huna would leave the good life he had in
Babylonia. But he did, and when Rabbi Hiyya told Rabbi
the news, Rabbi's face turned white, fearing that he had
ensnared himself. Then Rabbi Hiyya clarified the matter: it
was not Rav Huna the man who was coming to Israel; it was
his coffin. He came only to be buried in Israel, not to live
there. Because he caused this embarrassing misunderstand-
ing, Rabbi Hiyya temporarily retired from the Bet Hava'ad
(Committee of Scholars) and for thirty days he abstained
from entering Rabbi's home. Rabbi Hiyya was one of the
very few who did come from Babylonia to settle permanently in Israel.

On the matter of purity of lineage and the relative value
of Jews in Babylonia versus those in Israel, Rabbi Yochanan
was much more easy-going. He was accustomed to sending
his own messenger and other scholars to Babylonia to maintain communications between the yeshivas of both countries, and he is said to have rebuked those of his pupils who
mocked the Babylonians. Yet even he became the victim of
discrimination. A second-generation *amora* in Babylonia,
Ze'iri, who made *aliyah* to Israel in the middle of the third

century, declined Rabbi Yochanan's offer of his daughter in marriage. Ze'iri avoided him at every opportunity so as not to have to face him and tell him that he did not trust the purity of the genealogy of the Israeli people, even if this was the daughter of the second- generation genius. When the two happened to walk together and arrived at a water crossing, Ze'iri carried Rabbi Yochanan on his shoulders to make sure he would not get wet. The latter asked him sarcastically: "Our Torah is kosher, but our daughters are not?"

How ironical it is that the supporters of the Babylonian Exile began at that period to suddenly recall the claim of Ezra's time regarding the faulty families of Israel. They forgot that they themselves or their parents had arrived in Babylonia from Israel. And of course Rabbi Judah Ha-Nasi, whose ancestry dates from Hillel Habavli (Hillel, the Babylonian), reacted gravely to criticism of Jewish lineage in Israel and declared that he saw faults in the Babylonian Jews' family pedigrees.

The assertive Rabbi determined on his death bed that in Babylonia there is a place called Humanya, whose people are all bastards, and in a place called Birka there are two brothers who swapped wives, and in another place, called Birta *destiya*, they used to fish on Saturdays, thus not observing the ways of God, until they were banished by Rabbi ben Rabbi Yoshiya. He also said of the population of Shechnatziv that they were clowns (Babylonian Talmud, *Pesachim*).

Indeed these condemnations by Rabbi appear only in the Babylonian Talmud and not in the Jerusalem one. This is probably what the Babylonians thought was being said in Israel as they continued to pursue religious preeminence in Babylonia. After Rabbi's death they set up the yeshivas

of Sura, Pumbedita, and Nehardea, the latter headed by
Shmuel.

The Babylonian Jews did not even accept the Jews who
lived nearby. The Babylonian Talmud saw them as inferior
and rejected them because they did not observe the family
purity laws, and their ancestry wasn't pure as well (*Kiddushin*). Babylonia was considered, from this aspect, "whole-
some," containing no disqualified Jews. Michan, or Mishan
in the Jerusalem Talmud (a region located in present-day
Iraq), was "dead" because all its inhabitants were disqualified, and Maday was "sick" because some of its Jews were
disqualified, and Eylam was dying. And what was the difference between the sick and the dying? The sick came back
to life, but the dying died.

So the people of Mishan turned to Israel for counsel on
halakhic matters instead of to the nearby Babylonia. In one
case they asked Rabbi whether they were allowed to sail on
the sea for trade purposes, despite their ancestors' vow not
to leave the land. Rabbi's answer was that they should carry
on as their ancestors had, and avoid seafaring. The Mishan
community also sent some of its dead to be buried in Israel,
evidence of which can be seen today on graves found in Bet
She'arim, the burial place of Rabbi himself.

Rabbi Yitzhak said the Babylonian scholars were so bitter
toward their Israeli counterparts that they created the ruling
that if one lives in Babylonia, it is as if he lives in Israel, and
therefore he must not leave it (*Ketubot* 11a).

The dispute between Babylonia and Israel regarding those
disqualified for marriage, with each accusing the other of
impure blood, stopped only thanks to the intervention of Ula,
a friend of Rabbi Abahu. The Talmud recounts that when

Ula visited Rabbi Yehuda in Babylonia, he saw that his son, Rabbi Yitzchak, had not married. When he asked him why, the answer was that he was concerned about the problem of ancestry. The Israelis' charge of tainted ancestry—that the longer Jews remained in Babylonia the more their pedigree declined—had penetrated the extremely religious in Babylonia. At the same time, they could not choose a bride from Israel, because it was said about them that they were impure in comparison with those from Babylonia. Hence there was a risk that many Jews would refuse to have a family.

Ula reacted strongly to this attitude and suggested that Rabbi Yehuda and his son stop picking at the history of six hundred years—for example, there was a claim against Israel that they exchanged wives with each other—and check the quality of the present-day family to determine whether it is acceptable or not. As a result Ula and Rabbi Abahu, who was his partner in this effort, succeeded in avoiding dividing the nation.

It is clear that no love was lost between the two Jewish communities. Some, like Resh Lakish, openly scoffed at the Babylonian Jews who came to Israel to study and then returned to Babylonia, blaming them for weakening Israel. Once he was swimming in the river Jordan and an ex-Babylonian, Rabbah bar bar Hana, offered his hand. Resh Lakish rejected it, saying: "I hate you all (Babylonians); not only did you not come to Israel with Ezra, you also keep coming and going and never remain here. If you would have come all together with Ezra, you would have constituted a strong wall free of decay, but since you come separately, you are like wooden doors that get decayed."

Rabbi Yochanan of Israel was less aggressive. He sent a

messenger to Rav Yehuda in Babylonia to convey the Torah studies. They agreed about many things except about the value of Israel and Babylonia. Rav Yehuda, who refused to feel guilty for Israel's fading hegemony, would say that anyone who makes *aliyah* to Israel breaches a mandatory commandment, basing his words on the verse *Bavela yuva'u veshama yichyu ad yom pokdi otam,* "They will be brought to Babylonia and remain there until I redeem them." Rav Yehuda even went further, citing the Babylonian Shmuel, who said that just as it is forbidden to leave Israel, so it is forbidden to leave Babylonia to go to any other country, suggesting that although living in Babylonia is living in exile, it is not like all the other exiles. Egypt, for instance, was considered a dark exile. Babylonia, which had Torah-studying yeshivas, was similar to Israel; it was not a dark exile but an illuminating one.

At the time the greatness of the Israeli yeshivas was still in existence, Rabbi Yochanan had brilliant students, some of whom arrived from Babylonia, and they continued to create their own work.

Rabbi Yochanan voiced his opinion about the meagerness of Babylonian scholarship, at one point reacting to a rumor brought to him by Rabbi Zaki, who was originally from Babylonia but eventually came to study in Israel. When Zaki said, "An Amonite woman, daughter of a converted Amonite man, is 'kosher,' while a daughter of a converted Amonite woman is unacceptable," Rabbi Yochanan said, "You have made this up," saying that the rumor was unauthorized, fictitious, and adding that a Babylonian remains a Babylonian. Elsewhere he tells Rabbi Hiyya ben Ba "(only) two things [*halakhot*] you have succeeded in" (Jerusalem Talmud, *Suka*

4a), meaning that only two rulings on *halakhah* made by the Babylonian Torah center met with Israeli agreement. Not much of a yield!

Tension between sages of the two Torah centers was not uncommon. A rumor regarding the work at the Temple on Yom Kippur attributed to Rabbah, the Babylonian sage, was brought before Rabbi Yirmiyah of the Land of Israel, who was famous for his sharp tongue. (The latter had arrived there from Babylonia but had since considered himself an Israeli.) He was also well known for his line of pointed questions, the purpose of which was to find and emphasize the border cases of the *halakhah*, a characteristic that more than once irritated his Israeli teachers, who were not prepared for this kind of a discussion. Of the rumor he remarked: "Stupid Babylonians! [in Aramaic *Bavlai Tipshai*] Because they live in a dark [geographically low] land, their *halakhot* are dark [low] as well." In the debate following the issue, Rabbah goes on to tell his friend, "Until now we were called "stupid" and now we shall be called "the stupidest stupids.""

Babylonia was perceived by the Israeli sages as "the rock bottom of the world" (Jerusalem Talmud, *Berachot* 4a*). As many of the sages in the Holy Land thought that the genuine tradition of the *halakhah* belonged to the Israeli sages, at least in certain historical periods, they more than once rejected Babylonian versions of *halakhot* as unfounded.

However, one must not forget that the term "Babylonian" is a generalization with a negative emotional load. This attribute is part of the criticism of Babylonian rulings and at times may turn the concrete *halakhic* debate away from its real essence. Surprisingly, the Babylonian sages accepted this attitude in good humor, because in principle they agreed that one of the Israeli sages is worth two of the Babylonian, although not everyone felt that way.

Israeli scholars, such as Rabbi Eliezer ben Shamo'a and Rabbi Yochanan Ha-Sandlar, the cobbler, no longer had a pride of place in Israel and said they wanted to go to Babylonia to study there. Although ultimately they remained in Israel, their intention points to the loss of the Israel's scholarly authority.

The Israeli scholars who fought to retain control of the fixing of the calendar recognized that they did not dare lose this power. However, they ceded authority in other matters of leadership. Rabbi—whose stature in Israel was so highly regarded that he was almost a monarch—agreed to appoint Rabbi Hiyya ben Nathan as *av bet din*, the chairman of the court (Sanhedrin), and as such his deputy in Babylonia, suggesting that between the rebellion's end and the beginning of the *amoraim* period the Israeli leadership had been so weakened that it had to lean on a figure from the Diaspora.

A cynical paragraph in the Jerusalem Talmud (*Ta'anit* 84), however, indicates that Rabbi did not entirely accept the Babylonian leadership. He refused to give Rav Hanina bar Hama (another Hanina) a *semikhah,* in effect declining to ordain him, because Hanina had corrected him in public, perhaps with the intention of shaming him. Rabbi was furious and asked Rav Hanina to name the source of this correction. Rav Hanina replied: Rav Himnuna of Babylonia. So Rabbi told Hanina to let Rav Himnuna appoint him as a sage.

The Jerusalem Talmud recounts a story indicating that, despite the growing gap between the Israeli and the Babylonian scholars, Rabbi kept good relations not only with the

Roman Caesar Antoninus but also with King Artaban, who was the last of the Parthian dynasty and reigned in 213–224 BCE. In one story, the king sent Rabbi a priceless precious stone and asked him to send him back an item of equal value. Rabbi sent him a mezzuza. The king was dismayed and told him: I sent you something priceless and you sent me something worth a single coin? Rabbi replied: You sent me something that I have to guard, but I sent you something that will guard you even in your sleep (*Pe'a*).

We know that Rabbi commanded great respect, so much so that communities in Babylonia still turned to him for guidance. Once the people of Nineveh posed an unusual question. They wanted to pray for rain in a dry summer, but prayers for rain are said in the winter. In which of the eighteen blessings of the "standing" prayers (*Shmone Esrei Berachot*) should they incorporate it?

We also know that Babylonians sent gifts to Rabbi, as confirmed by one of the messengers who carried the Israeli Torah to Babylonia and returned with a delivery of artichokes for Rabbi from a rich Jew by the name of Ben Bonyes, who lived in Nausa (Babylonian Talmud, *Eruvin*).

However, despite the love and respect accorded Rabbi, he couldn't halt the growing Babylonian independence, which was further strengthened when he finalized the Mishnah, and the Babylonian sages, headed by Rav, who set up the Sura Yeshiva, began to debate on the Mishnah in the Torah-study centers they established there. This was the beginning of the Babylonian Talmud, which eventually overtook the Jerusalem Talmud and shaped the living customs of the People of Israel with all their complexities.

· 7 ·

THE END OF THE ISRAELI
TORAH CENTER

*A*FTER THE CODIFICATION of the Jerusalem Talmud and on the threshold of the Babylonian Talmud's being codified, there is only one known case of an address that was made to Israel by Babylonia concerning a certain *halakhah*. After the codification of the Babylonian Talmud, Israel was scorned mainly by the middle *gaonim* in Babylonia, who aggressively tried to impose the Babylonian Talmud and customs on Israel. The most forceful one was Rav Yehudai Gaon in the seventh and eighth centuries. Head of the Sura Yeshiva, he made instructions and even the customs of the Babylonian yeshivas compulsory for Israeli *halakhot*. There was a power struggle between the two centers, with Israel repeatedly rejecting the Babylonian imposition, arguing that life in Israel is *lived according to our forefathers and everything is written in the books*. However, Rav Yehudai did not relent until Israel was forced into agreeing and eventually accepting all the Babylonian interpretation and customs.

Strangely, throughout the generations we don't see any complaints by the Israeli scholars about traditions and customs of the Babylonian Jewry. On the contrary, theirs was a forgiving attitude. For example, regarding the case of the High Priest and the king in the Temple, the Jerusalem Talmud asks, "but there, in Babylonia, they bring the Torah to the Exilarch?" and Rabbi Yossi, son of Rabbi Bun, answers complacently and with historical respect, "Because David's seed is planted in him and therefore they treat him as was the custom of their ancestors."

In some vital national political issues, an abyss opens between the Israeli and the Babylonian scholars, such as in the interpretation of the division of the kingdom and the land into two parts by Jeroboam ben Nevat during the reign of Rechavam, a split that must have been a national shock. It is told in I Kings (11:29) that on the way from Jerusalem, the prophet Achiya met Jeroboam, who was wearing a new robe. The prophet ripped the robe into twelve pieces, symbolizing the twelve tribes of Israel, and gave ten to Jeroboam, leaving two to Rechavam, the son of Solomon. Thus the Land of Israel was divided into two kingdoms (Samaria and Judea). All the Israeli scholars harshly criticized Jeroboam ben Nevat and Achiya Hashiloni, his "cheerleader" (not however, Rabbi Yochanan, whose statement is half-for and half-against). The Babylonian *amoraim*, like Rav Nachman, on the other hand, commented on the "new robe":

"The same as a new robe, which is flawless, so is Jeroboam's Torah," and the word "new" is taken to mean that it has been revised, that is, it contains things unheard before.

Another incident is found in the following story about *orlah,* or the prohibition in Israel from eating the fruit of a tree in the first three years of its growth. In *Kiddushin* tractate (39a), the sharp scholars of Pumbedita in Babylonia said that there is no *orlah* abroad. The Babylonian Rav Yehuda delivered this question to Rabbi Yochanan in Israel, who aggressively answered that anyone who says that there is no *orlah* abroad will have no grandchild or great grandchild. This warning was particularly directed to Rav Yehuda. Thus Pumbedita's attempt to free Babylonia from carrying out an Israeli-dependent mitzvah failed.

Another attempt was made by the Babylonian Rav Yoseph to deny Rabbi Evyatar, a well-known pupil of Rabbi Yochanan, the authority to rule on divorce matters of men who came from Babylonia to Israel. The *aliyah* of Babylonian Jews to Israel had bred many domestic tragedies and social and economic problems. Yet the following story shows an almost ideal interaction between Babylonia and Israel, which initially indicates respect on both sides but in the end provides a result in which Israel is held to be lesser than Babylonia.

An important rabbi in one of Babylonia's small towns complained that bad rumors were being spread about him; he was suspected of prostitution. Rav Yehuda couldn't decide whether to banish him (what if the local rabbis in town needed him?) or not to banish him, thus risking blasphemy. By chance he met an Israeli a*mora,* who advised him to follow Rabbi Yochanan's previous ruling that "if the suspected rabbi looks like an angel of God, people will want to learn from him, but if he doesn't, they will not." So Rav Yehuda banished him. After a time Rav Yehuda fell ill and among those who visited him was the same suspected rabbi. Rav Yehuda smiled when he saw him. The suspected person became irritated and said, "Isn't it enough that you banished me, you also laugh at me?" To which Rav Yehuda replied, "I smiled only because now that I am going to the next world, I am glad that I did not flatter even a great man like you."

After the death of Rav Yehuda, this same rabbi went to the Bet Midrash (study hall) in Babylonia and asked to be released from the banishment. He was told that in Babylonia there was no person as great as Rav Yehuda, so he should go to Rabbi in Israel, who would free him. The man did as he was told; then Rabbi asked Rabbi Ami to check the man's case and told him to let him off if he thought he deserved it. However, when Rabbi Zira raised an objection, the banishment was not lifted.

Although it seems from this case that terms of reciprocation existed between Israel and Babylonia, if we look into it carefully we discover otherwise. In Babylonia this person was banished by Rav Yehuda only after he found support in a ruling by the Israeli Rabbi Yochanan. And his banishment was left in place by scholars in Israel despite the fact that Rabbi Ami leaned toward releasing him. The fact was that the scholars in Israel who refused to release him were originally from Babylonia and did not want to blemish the good memory of their teacher and friend Rav Yehuda in particular and of Babylonia in general. The story ends with the banished man's unnatural death, which seems to justify the Babylonian banishment. One can deduce that in this case the Israeli opinion was less important than the Babylonian.

THE FAILURE OF *ALIYAH*

One of the most interesting questions applies to the period of six hundred years preceding the Second Exile to Babylonia. How did it happen that the First Return to Zion (*Shivat Zion*) succeeded, whereas the Second Return was much less successful? Those who contributed to the success of the First Return were members of the institution of *halakhic* authority called *Anshey Knesset Hagdola,* the Great Public Assembly (also known as the Great Synagogue) as well as two major historical figures, Ezra and Nechemia (Nehemiah).

In the Talmud there is a beautiful legend regarding what happened in the Great Public Assembly that took place on Rosh Hashanah after the First Return to Zion. At this assembly, people physically captured the drive toward paganism (*Avodah Zarah,* or idol worship) and eliminated it. They also wanted to eliminate the sexual drive but acknowledged that it was vital for life, so they only blinded it.

Why did they need to do this? The reason was that both at the time of Ezra, as well as six hundred years later, the elite of the nation who refused to go to Israel justified their decision by the same strange argument that if they went to Israel they would be tempted to perform pagan rituals. They said that the First Temple was destroyed as a result of pagan worship by the Jews, which led to their exile from Israel, and they were not prepared to experience this again.

To argue against this allegedly religious excuse to avoid immigration to Israel because of the fear of paganism among the Jews, the people of the Knesset Hagdola explained that "the reward is according to the effort," which in this case means that even if the hypocritical make the claim that Israel increases the libido, their own righteousness will surmount it.

However, the people feigned innocence again, saying they didn't want to take the risk. The great national leaders of the time, headed by Ezra Hasofer (*hasofer* means "the scribe"), who was concerned solely with the good of the nation, sensed the gravity of the situation. If the people didn't seize the opportunity to return to Zion, the result would be national disaster. And if all the religious and intellectual powers were not mobilized for this purpose, the people of Israel would be divided and eventually disintegrate. To quiet opposition to the Return to Zion, the institution of Anshey Knesset Hagdola was established ad hoc to press for the return of the exiles.

The leaders also coped with the second claim of those who opposed the Return to Zion that all the privileged families were in Babylonia while only the questionable ones were left in Israel. This rationale recalls the argument of the recent generation of Orthodox Jewry who refused to come to modern-day Israel because "the state of its religion is very poor." The Knesset Hagdola people decided to takes steps to eliminate this excuse. Wherever possible, they purified all the doubtful families and sent away all the foreign wives rather than let them convert and remain. At that time there was a rule that women must wear *sinorim* (literally "aprons," but in this case they mean undergarments) lest their private parts be exposed during housework, thus eliminating possible incest. In this way, the Knesset Hagdola removed the sting of the naysayers' claims, and afterward the Jewish population in Israel increased greatly.

Incidentally, Ezra Hasofer, who was the greatest leader of his generation, postponed his immigration in order to wait for the death of Baruch ben Neria, who was too sick to travel to Israel. Ezra feared that if he left Baruch ben Neria in Babylonia, a dishonest pupil might exploit Baruch's stay there to remain in exile.

Ezra, who did not leave a loophole for the people with selfish interests, created a religious and national consensus regarding the *aliyah* to Israel. His success is in sharp contrast to the weakness of the Babylonian leadership, who failed to take action when the nation's fate was at risk. Avraham Korman ("Deciphering Legends," Tel-Aviv, 1991) emphasizes the ability of the Knesset Hagdola to transfer the hegemony of Babylonia to Israel as a religious and national center, and to make the Babylonians acknowledge this shift.

In opposition to the people of the Knesset Hagdola, the Babylonian leaders began to develop their own megalomania over those who fought hard to preserve the hegemony of Israel.

Professor Yehezeiel Kaufman described the differences between the First and the Second Exiles: The first exiles were uprooted from their homes; many of them were born in Babylonia and did not know Jerusalem. They had integrated themselves in the economic and cultural society of the locals and considered themselves Babylonians. Life was good; there were no special rules against them. Anti-Semitism did not exist then. Yet, despite all this, they agreed to leave their Babylonian homes and make *aliyah*, returning to Israel, the land of their forefathers. They had discovered the siren call of their nationality even within the Babylonian Exile.

How did it happen that the First Return was a success, whereas the Second, a few hundred years later, was so meager? Was their monotheistic belief not dominant enough? The first returners entered an environment so paganistic that they needed the Knesset Hagdola to neutralize the symbols of idolatry, after which the large flow of returners to Israel began.

The Knesset Hagdola also succeeded in denouncing those who became wealthy from dealing with religious and holy matters. The members of the Knesset held twenty-four fasts in order to neutralize the impact of these influence peddlers. They cited Shmaya in the tractate on ethical teachings (*Pirkei Avot*), who said, "Love work and hate the Rabbinate," adding that if the rabbis give advice only for money and not for altruistic purposes, they are not interpreting the Torah correctly.

In later periods of the exile, the leadership was not successful in eliminating the influence of this wealthy class, and it was these people who influenced the Babylonian Jews to remain there.

In contrast to the well-being of the Babylonian Jews, Israel suffered under suppression, its wealth drained, with no help from Babylonia. But the Babylonian Jewry remained indifferent. Only a small number, approximately five thousand, returned to Israel in the Second Return to Zion with Ezra in 458 BCE, while at the same time hundreds of thousands of Jews remained in Babylonia. In the First Return to Zion with Zrubavel in 538 BCE, fifty thousand (including more than seven thousand slaves) arrived in Israel.

It seems that the Babylonian Jewry believed they fulfilled their duty by contributing some of their members to the

Shivat Zion, and for the next four hundred years they took care of their own needs and interests. After the destruction of the Second Temple (70 CE), the Jewish population in Israel and in Babylonia was almost equal. The only thing that changed after the crushing of the Bar Kokhba rebellion (132 CE) was that *aliyah* dwindled to a trickle, and whereas before both single people and families had come to Israel, afterward many Jews fled to Babylonia, including scholars. This immigration of scholars to Babylonia contained a fertile grain for the development of the Jewish community in Babylonia.

In 393 the Roman Empire under Theodosius, who had made Christianity the state religion, prohibited marriage in Israel according to the Jewish law, an action directed toward further diminishing the Jewish population. This was the first in a chain of edicts of prohibitions and punishments in the form of taxes, subjections, and prohibitions both by the Western Roman Empire and the Eastern Empire—Byzantium—on Jewish communities all over the empire. The result, as one would expect, was to increase flight from Israel, mainly to Babylonia.

On the brink of the fifth century, the Sanhedrin in Israel and the Bet Midrash were ruined, their scholars either killed or hiding in caves for fear of Roman legions. This state of affairs gave birth to the beginning of the spiritual ascent of the Babylonian Jews. It had begun with the Babylonian scholars studying in Israel mainly in the great times of Rabbi Judah Ha-Nasi, and it continued with the *Yerida,* the emigration of Jews, some of them to Babylonia, like Rabbi Hiyya (also called Rabbah), who was close to Rabbi. He and Shmuel both set up large yeshivas in Babylonia. It took another two hundred years before Babylonia became the spiritual stronghold it eventually was, although it owed its greatness to the Land of Israel.

The responsibility of Babylonia and any guilt it felt for the rapid decline of Israel in this sad period is an unsolved question. However, it is a fact that the Jewish community in Babylonia dwelt in wealth and comfort while the *Yishuv,* the local settlement in Israel, fought with the remains of its force for its existence without any outside help. Babylonia continued to struggle to obtain complete reign over the spiritual leadership of the Jewish people and the Land of Israel, which took them another five hundred years to achieve.

In addition to their haughty attitude toward the Israeli sages, the Babylonian Jews also had their own internal disputes, controversies, and crises. One of the battles was between Daniel and David, respective heads of the yeshivas in Sura and Pumbedita, regarding the appointment of a new exilarch when Daniel tried to depose Rav Avraham ben Sherira Gaon from heading the Pumbedita Yeshiva.

An additional crisis came upon the Sura Yeshiva at the beginning of the seventh century when, because of the absence of a suitable personality, the *gaon* chair remained empty for more than two years after the death of Rav Moshe Kahana, who had headed it for ten years. At the time, the exilarch, Mar Ukva, instead of rescuing the yeshiva from destruction, chose to transfer the income from the taxes of its district—Horasan—into his own personal treasury. Eventually in 842 a new *gaon,* Rav Cohen Zedek, was appointed and he fought strongly against Ukva's usurpation. The Jewish administrators in Baghdad were finally forced to appeal to the Babylonian authorities and ask them to distance Mar Ukva from the center of public life. The Khalif expelled him and he was obliged to leave Baghdad and move to Karaman-sha, east of Baghdad. But this was not the end of it. Ukva was a very gifted and knowledgeable as well as a shifty man, and he used an opportunity to flatter the Khalif with a song of praise in pure literary Arabic and thus won his heart. The Khalif agreed to let Ukva return to his old post in Baghdad. Only after twenty years, during the time of Rav Amram Gaon, was this conniving person finally deposed as exilarch and dispatched to Kairouan, where he was very welcome. Ukva's story is an example of the turbulent relations inside the Babylonian Jewish community that eventually reduced its strength and fame.

During the time of the *geonim* the economic structure of the Jewish community in Babylonia underwent changes. Because of various pressures by the authorities, the Jewish farmers had to abandon agriculture as a source of living and gradually began moving into towns and hamlets, making their living now from trade and craftsmanship. The land which used to be a man's basic and most valued source of living and asset was abandoned, and this negative process undoubtedly turned Babylonia into a "normal exile" like the rest of the countries so typical of the Jewish Diaspora, lacking natural roots in their land of dwelling. The abandonment of agricultural regions caused the eventual destruction of old Jewish settlements in Babylonia such as Nahar Pakud, Shalchi, and others. Babylonian Jews thus became a landless class, a fact that changed their traditional socioeconomic relations.

But the change came too late for the Israeli scholars. In the first half of the tenth century Babylonia and not Israel received the right to fix the calendar, after a bitter and lengthy struggle between Rav Saadyah, head of the Sura Yeshiva in Babylonia, and Rabbi Aharon ben Meir, head of the Tiberias Yeshiva in the Land of Israel. The result was a split into two peoples and two schools, which celebrated the holidays on different days. Eventually, however, everybody, including the Israeli Jews, accepted the Babylonian calendar as the prevailing one.

This incident was one of the salient signs of division between Babylonia and Israel and contributed to the spiritual and social distancing of the two communities.

It was said, "The head was in Israel and the body in Babylonia." This tragic and strange state of affairs could not last forever, and Babylonia managed to mount the head over the body while Israel was weak and poor. Babylonia had become the spiritual leader and Israel weakened and stepped off the stage.

We can be cynical and say the beginning of Babylonia's victory over the Land of Israel derives from the Golden Rule: whoever has the gold makes the rules. It's a fact that the Babylonian community increased in every generation and, with it, its wealth and plenty, while Israel lost all its material power under the pressure of subjugation and enormous taxes, and thus its leadership was defeated.

Israel's loss was Babylonia's gain. While Jewish Babylonia prospered, time and again Israel was crushed under different conquests. Fortunately the vital spiritual cord was never cleft. Its legacy was immense: The Holy Scriptures contain twenty-four books, as well as some more external books—the Mishnah and all its large external literature; the Jerusalem Talmud and all the midrashic literature in the *halakhah* and *aggadah*, as well as the apocalyptic-messianic literature of which a small part was recently discovered in foreign languages in caves and other archeological sites in the State of Israel.

However, one must not forget that while Babylonia perhaps had sinned against Israel, politically and nationally, it also embraced the entire legacy that was left by Israeli scholars, and it preserved and nurtured this faithfully.

Nevertheless, a nation cannot be revived unless it is on its own land. And the hope of returning one day to Israel never died and was eternalized in the phrase: *Le'shana ha'ba'a bi-Ye rushalayim,* "Next year in Jerusalem," which ends each Passover seder and is recited in the daily prayer *Tefilat Shmone Esrei* and the *Birkat Hamazon (Grace after meals).* Babylonia held well through three large and consecutive periods of the *amoraim,* the *savoraim,* and the *geonim,* but it too failed and ultimately came to an end.

PART TWO

· 8 ·

Two Talmuds:
Two Schools of Thought

*A*LTHOUGH THE TALMUD at first looks disorderly and inconsistent, it was actually put together in a very concise and accurate manner, the editors making sure to include all the authentic sources and mentions of every doubtful case. The citations and arguments are classified and distinguished according to the source (Mishnah, *baraita,* or *amora's* opinion). There is also a special marking of the kinds of questions, and a distinction is made between the various questions, refutes, and those contradictions and difficulties still open to be solved. Also there is a meaning to the order in which the items are presented, that applies to the weight of a possible solution.

124 •

This accuracy of the editing work, which is the fruit of generations of work, made the Talmud very consistent and open to fixed methods of study and interpretation. Its editing work caused the Talmud, which is strictly speaking not a book of laws, to serve as a first-class legal source, and thanks to the strictness of its method of thought as well as its writing and style of expression, to continue to be created in subsequent generations as well.

An interesting difference between the two Talmuds is reflected in their attitude toward the Hasmonean Rebellion (led by Judah Maccabee) and attempts to divert the focus of the Hanukkah holiday from the heroic figures of the Hasmoneans toward the divine miraculous aspect. And indeed the Babylonian Talmud depicts the history of Israel from the Hasmonean Rebellion up to the failure of Bar Kokhba, citing reconciliation trends with the foreign rulers and expressing reservations about war and rebellion.

The authentic Israeli tradition is reflected in the Jerusalem Talmud. It sees the rebellion as just and avoids condemning the rebels, and also it does not contain any reconciliatory remarks about the victorious enemy. It does not demand avoidance of any unconditional objection and actual deeds.

In contrast, the Babylonian Talmud displays a passive and antirevolutionary attitude, consistent adjustment to the conditions of exile and continued subjection. The Babylonian Talmud does not mention initiated rebellions in order not to mention *erida Bamakhut*, the rebellion of the rulers, and the breaching of the explicit prohibition to *Lid'chok et Haketz* (to speed up Redemption). There are no revolutionary movements in the Babylonian Talmud that sweep the multitudes, no messianic slogans, and no public leadership that evokes rebellion. In contrast, the Jerusalem Talmud does not see the story of Hanukkah, for example, as a simple victory but rather as a symbol of the triumph of spiritual light over darkness.

Zilka's Distinctions between the Two Talmuds

In her research for *Through the Eye of the Jerusalem Talmud's Legends* (*Be'eyn Agadot Hayerushalmi*, Beyt Morasha, Tashsat [1999]), Dr. Yaffa Zilka deals mainly with the issue of legends in the Jerusalem Talmud as against those in the Babylonian Talmud, retrospectively examining the formation of the Jerusalem Talmud as a point of departure.

The Jerusalem Talmud was edited in the Land of Israel around the year 400 in the town of Tiberias. However, it was not edited and codified in an orderly manner. Various tractates were edited in different centers in Israel, namely in Zippori, Caesaria, and Lod, and all under permanent pressure of war, occupation, decrees of forcible conversion, as well as poverty and want.

The reasons why the Jerusalem Talmud remained in Israel and did not succeed in reaching outside its borders were historical and political. Even in Israel it was almost neglected after its conclusion, because of the lack of interest in it. Its manuscripts gradually became rare and this fact continues to remove it from memory.

Simultaneously with the rising importance of the Jewish center in Babylonia, the Jerusalem Talmud was pushed aside and eventually replaced by the undisputed Babylonian Talmud. In contrast to the Jerusalem Talmud, the Talmud that was codified in Babylonia around the year 500 developed in a relaxed historical, social, religious, and economic environment. It acquired many manuscripts and was widely and consistently distributed among all the Jewish communities. Because of its organization and editing work, distribution, and accessibility, the Babylonian Talmud had acquired a consistent interpretational tradition, both early and late, from two important groups: the *savoraim*—"expositors," the rabbis who came after the *tannaim* and the *amoraim* and who worked on the final redaction of the Talmud; and the *geonim*—the spiritual leaders of the Jews, who were presidents of the Babylonian yeshivas in Sura and Pumbedita. This tradition has not stopped from the moment of its final codification up to today. During the time of the *geonim,* the Babylonian Talmud became the chief accepted and authoritative source of *halakhah* for the entire Jewish community, so much so that Rav Sherira Gaon, in his famous epistle devoted to the history of the Oral Torah literature, does not even mention the existence of the Jerusalem Talmud.

In later generations the Jerusalem Talmud was almost forgotten, its distribution and number of manuscripts became rarer and rarer, a fact that has been testified to by the heads of the Babylonian Period (about 1001 CE) who complained of the absence of its copies, or of its errors, thereby justifying the lack of study of and reference to it.

Zilka claims in her research that we know very little about the Jerusalem Talmud during a period of more than five hundred years, from its codification at the end of the fourth century up to the beginning of the tenth century, and even after that, news about it is very meager. Furthermore, the Jerusalem Talmud was published in Venice in 1523, using the Leiden Manuscript of 1289, which is the only complete manuscript in existence. To our knowledge, there is no other composition in all the classic scholarly literature that depends entirely on the existence of a single manuscript. Yet this is the case with the Jerusalem Talmud. Without the Leiden Manuscript, the Jerusalem Talmud would have disappeared entirely, never to be published for our examination today. The very fact of its continued existence leans on a single surviving document, which even its owner admitted "contains errors."

Above all, the absence of examination and interpretation of the Jerusalem Talmud caused an even greater problem: the lack of a consistent tradition of understanding the Jerusalem Talmud. Only exceptional individuals have had the opportunity to study it for any length of time. Therefore, as a rule the Jerusalem Talmud has no comprehensible interpretation, and of course no developing interpretational tradition, a fact that makes its study in depth very difficult indeed.

For these reasons, the Babylonian Talmud continues to be considered the central textbook, a textbook that is orderly, systematical, and well edited, referring to issues discussed and examined through a wide scope. By contrast, the Jerusalem Talmud is seen as a forgotten, unfinished, and disorderly book, one that only very few study, and for those who do, its main role is to serve as a reference and source of comparison to clarify issues in the Babylonian Talmud.

However, Zilka's study postulates that the difference between the two Talmuds lies not only in external, historical, and social contexts, but in a much more fundamental way. In the two Talmuds themselves there is an attempt to portray their differences. For instance, the Babylonian Talmud contains a story about Rav Zira, who, before making *aliyah* to Israel, prepared himself carefully and fasted a hundred fasts so that he could forget the Babylonian way of study before he approached that of the Israelis. The explanation given is that in the Babylonian Talmud the student is like a man who walks in the dark and looks for something, through many hardships, until he finally finds it; while in the Jerusalem Talmud everything is lit, clear, and illuminating.

Rabbi Shneour Zalman of Lyady (*Ha'admor Hazaken*) explained the differences between the two schools of thought this way: The study of the Babylonian Talmud involves questions and sophistry and solving of contradictions, which is why it was said to be "done in darkness," while the study of the Jerusalem Talmud is done in a state of light, and that is why Rabbi Zira was obliged to forget his Babylonian studies.

From this essential difference between the two Talmuds, Zilka's work contends that a parallel difference also exists with regard to their *aggadah* (legends) sections, which she says also are essentially different.

In his introduction to *The Way of the Torah*, Naftali Zvi Yehuda Berlin (the *Natziv*) discusses two different concepts and approaches to studying the Torah throughout the generations. He makes a distinction between the study of the Torah and the ruling of the *halakhah* through intuition and divine illumination (Jerusalem), versus through deep thought and analysis (Babylonian). He considers this disparity to be the difference between the Israeli Torah and the Babylonian Torah: "and when they came to Babylon they had to be more careful with King Josiah's warning not to teach unless they investigate and deepen first into the common *halakhah* and from it rule about the uncommon *halakhah*, as was taught by King Solomon, since in Israel they enjoyed the privilege of its light, which reduced their need of study, something that was not the case in Babylon. Babylon is a darkened depth which can be lit only through a great quibbling and minute study (*pilpul*)."

Rav Kook, the Natziv's student, thought that this difference was due to "the Spirit of Holiness" which is so plentiful in Israel. Since Israel was closer to the living spirit of God, it affected, extended, and enlightened understanding of the *halakhot*. Abroad the impurity of the air and the soil inhibited it.

Between Salvation and Change

Zilka notes that Rav Kook speaks of another factor when he distinguishes between creation developed on exile ground and one nourished by the original source. "The standing light of Salvation is the Jerusalem Talmud, while the Babylonian Talmud is the light of Change, of the dark sitting in the land of darkness." Defining salvation versus change, Kook positioned the study of the Torah that takes the source of its inspiration from the very air of Israel, and the change that replaces that source with a translation, replacing it with a light that comes from the darkness of exile. "The letters of the Torah can be taken by hand and transferred from one place to another; however, the spiritual soul of the Torah can be felt only in its native place—in Israel."

Because the Israeli perspective examines life from an inner, intuitive point of view, it receives everything by a "straight light" from above, making it basically short and clear. In contrast, the Babylonian perspective, which examines things from the outside, necessitates much questioning, disputes, and solutions through analysis and weighing. It lacks the inner touch and thus the inner unity. Therefore the Babylonian Talmud's style is characterized by multiple details and lengthiness.

Illustrating the difference between *halakho*t in the two Talmuds is a story about Rabbi (Judah Ha-Nasi) and Rabbi Pinchas ben Ya'ir. The story begins with Rabbi, who wished to ease the life of the economically struggling Israeli farmers by allowing them to forego the sabbatical year (*shmita*); *shmita* required them to leave the farmland fallow for the seventh year of a seven-year growing cycle and to cease all agricultural activity. He addressed Rabbi Pinchas about this matter, but the latter disagreed with him because of his fanaticism, replying that the people can eat chicory for one year instead of wheat. Rabbi Pinchas was a zealot among the *tannaim* and observed the ancient *halakhah* without conceding to external circumstances, as opposed to Rabbi, who wished to compromise and thereby assist people to make their living.

When Rabbi learned of Rabbi Pinchas's response, he asked him to dine at his home. Rabbi Pinchas agreed, and Rabbi's face glowed with joy because Rabbi Pinchas was normally not known to enjoy what others offered. Rabbi Pinchas went on to explain his moral attitude to Rabbi: "Do you think that I wish to deprive Israel from pleasure? Israel is sacred. Some Israelis want to give to others but have nothing to give, and some have but do not want to give, and you want to give and you have. However, I am in a hurry now to perform a mitzvah [*Pidyon Shevu'im*—liberation of captives—an important and urgent mitzvah], and when I come back, I shall come to you."

When he came back, he entered through the entrance

where white mules were standing. The white mules were a strain of wild mules, strong and therefore dangerous, that were symbols of wealth. So Rabbi Pinchas said: "The Angel of Death is in his home. Shall I dine with him?"

Upon hearing that, Rabbi came out and told Rabbi Pinchas that he would sell the mules, castrate them, or slaughter them.

Rabbi Pinchas responded: "You shall not put an obstacle before a blind man. If you set them free, you will cause much damage (because they were wild beasts); if you castrate them, it is cruelty; if you kill them, it is cruelty as well as damage."

Rabbi tried talking to Rabbi Pinchas at length but failed. Then Rabbi cried and said, "Not only in their lifetime do they cause damage, after their death they cause even more."

Both Talmuds tell the story of a break in relations between the two men. However, each presents a different picture indicating their opposing spirit. In the Jerusalem Talmud, Rabbi concludes the dispute in a conciliatory tone with hope for cooperation in the world to come, while in the Babylonian Talmud, Rabbi cries out of his realization that their dispute will not be resolved in this world nor in the next one.

In the Babylonian Talmud, Rabbi Pinchas sees the white mules as emblematic of the status of Rabbi as the president of Israel. This status symbol is achieved by the keeping of dangerous and potentially injurious animals.

The story in the Jerusalem Talmud exposes an essential conflict between the *halakhic* or divine truth and its practical application, an unresolved issue in the limited present world. Rabbi Pinchas ben Ya'ir's faith is zealous and uncompromising, and he cannot accept an opposing opinion and therefore detaches its bearer from his surrounding environment and envelops him in a divine world in which he is protected by "heavenly fire." In the Jerusalem Talmud's story, Rabbi Pinchas is detached from Rabbi because of his own essence and not as a result of their conflict.

In contrast, in the Babylonian story the conflict is presented as a critique which does not come up against any opposing moral value and does not deal with a *halakhic* truth, where one would find it hard to compromise. The Babylonian author detached the dispute from its essential unsolvable root as it appears in the Jerusalem Talmud, and turned it into a moral issue whose value is clear to both parties, making the dispute external and interpersonal.

Another difference between the two attitudes comes to light. The Babylonian dispute is by its essence negating the opposing side and exposing its amorality. The Babylonian dispute does not collide with absolute truths, while the dispute in the Jerusalem Talmud—whose point of departure is in the absolute truth, which cannot be compromised—can be resolved because it is essentially true and sees the true fundamentals in its opposing opinions as well.

Rabbi in the Jerusalem story sees the tension between himself and Rabbi Pinchas as the different faces of the same truth, the truth which in the human reality seems divided but is really united and its unity will be realized again in the world to come.

The different endings of the two versions also draw a distinction between the Torah of Israel as against the Babylonian Torah. The Jerusalem *aggadah,* with its internal vision, penetrates the essence of contrasts and wishes to reconcile them, while the Babylonian *aggadah* hones, contrasts, and resolves situations in order to pronounce the ideological message it wishes to express.

Zilka points out that the two parallel stories are constructed on the same plot line and identical structure; however, despite their great external similarity, internally they differ, with each story built on different emphases leading in a different direction.

The Israeli story is deeply rooted in time and place. It introduces us to a difficult Israeli reality, which is struggling in real time to link the hard living reality with the demands of the pure *halakhah*. The narrator of the Jerusalem Talmud does not take sides in this conflict and presents it as humanly insolvable in the present world. However, the insolvable-to-date reality does not threaten the fundamental unified concept of the Israeli Torah, and at the end of the story Rabbi is sure that in the world to come, where the pure truth is examined, it will be possible to draw a link between the thinking of Rabbi and that of Rabbi Pinchas.

Therefore the Jerusalem *aggadah* reflects the complexity of the Israeli reality and is rooted in the needs of the present, but its heart is open to Heaven.

The Babylonian *aggadah* presents a different picture. The Babylonian narrator uses the elements of the Israeli story but takes them to very different places. This story turns an essentially Israeli conflict into a general moralistic conflict which fits every man and leader at any time and place. This is a conflict in which one party is right and the other acknowledges his own mistake. This story is built according to defined moral and social purposes and is meant to serve them.

The Jerusalem Talmud's *aggadah* tells the story in a way that penetrates directly into the heart of the event depicted, without introductions or conclusions. There within it, in a very defined place and time, in a few words and at times even without words or with a nonliteral reaction, it introduces us without any barriers into the event and the internal essence of the sage about whom it is speaking. Thus it enables us to penetrate into the nature of things, identify with them, and merge with their singular absoluteness.

The Babylonian Talmud's *aggadah* starts from a different point as well as time and place and aims to arrive at a different destination. The Babylonian sees ahead to an external and valued goal which it wishes to achieve. For this purpose it dismantles the event's unity from its internal aspect, introduces into it external factors that are to serve its purpose, and examines it from a wide ideological outlook while translating the actual story into concepts, principles, and points of view that will define and clarify general religious-ethical goals.

The story of Rabbi Akiva's death in the Jerusalem Talmud focuses on the actual capacity of an absolute selfless devotion, as against the issue in the Babylonian Talmud, which examines the relation between the Torah and its reward, and the meaning of the world to come. Another story in the Jerusalem Talmud teaches us what is true, deep devotion in prayer without any connection to the general ideological issue of the Babylonian Talmud, which deals with the ethical-value side of "The snake does not kill; it's the sin (that does)." King David in the Jerusalem Talmud teaches us what devotion is in the unceasing worship of God, as against the Babylonian Talmud's extended debate on King David's personality. Honi Ha-Me'agel in the Jerusalem version teaches us the essence of pining for the Temple and anticipating its construction, rather than the Babylonian ideological issue that discusses the character of study and the generation gap in study centers, and so forth.

The Jerusalem *aggadah* is more individual and therefore more humane, while the Babylonian *aggadah* exposes the work of the editor, who usually placed the story within a wide subject that examines it externally to arrive at an inclusive *halakhic* conclusion, which while important in itself, will never be able to illuminate the matter that created it.

This is a basic difference between both *aggadahs*. The Babylonian *aggadah* wishes to define clear issues of belief and ethics and does it through planned disputes into which are introduced additional characters with contrary ideas, the purpose of which is to sharpen and clarify its message. The Jerusalem's *aggadah* has an internal view that cannot be translated or dismantled and that is expressed in a concise formulation. It is important to note, though, that the Jerusalem *aggadah* does not ignore the complexity of the situations it presents. However, instead of creating external conflicts, it touches upon the internal aspect of the matter and from this point of view the opposites and their conciliation are expressed. When the story is depicted from within, it is perceived in its entirety and therefore it is definite, simple, and short. This element coincides with the conclusions of Rav Kook as to why he needed to purge himself of the Babylonian method of study before entering into the Jerusalem school in general.

The strength of the Jerusalem *aggadah* is also expressed in its dealing with the sages whom it describes. Both Talmuds tell a story about the same event and participating sages, but from a different perspective. The Jerusalem version sees

things from the character's interior: He is in a certain reality which is anchored in a certain time and place and he is
required to decide or act immediately. His decision is closely
linked with his singular personality and it stretches beyond
the current moment. The sages depicted in the Jerusalem are
super-pious, and their decisions and acts come from their
singularity and not out of an external and general formulation of values. Their action and decisions are the heart and
strength of the Jerusalem's *aggadah*. These scholars penetrate
our soul in a direct manner, leading us to an unknown destination in the worship of God.

The sages in the Babylonian lack this quality; the event
they experience becomes an external event, which is depicted
at length and is saturated with plot, tension, and extremity.
The main point seems to be a dispute between the sage and
other extreme characters, which serves as an ideological
debate with a conclusion. The Babylonian story detaches
the event from its original place and time, thus detaching it
from the sacredness of Israel and turning it into a story about
goals, values, and concepts. This approach also distances the
intimacy with the world of the sages of old.

But above all what differentiates the Jerusalem and the
Babylonian *aggadah*, according to Zilka, is the presence of
the Holy Land in the former, which at times is completely
erased when the story is transferred to the Babylonian. The
stories of the Jerusalem deal with matters that are strictly
connected to Israel, but in the Babylonian they are converted
to general ethical matters.

Another case in point is the story of the widow who
asked Rabbi Akiva if she could be released from the custom of a levirate marriage, which required her to marry her

brother-in-law. The story arose out of the complex historical-religious-human reality in Israel—for example, the need to maintain the family as a unit and to ensure the inheritance of land within the family—but in the Babylonian Talmud it became a purely *halakhic* event, detached from its origins. There are many more examples.

In conclusion, says Zilka, these are two parallel routes which contain the same contents, the same sages, the same values, but they create different essences. The Jerusalem's is Israeli while the other is Babylonian. The former shows the story from within, while the latter from without. The former arrives at the absolute; the latter illuminates a certain point in it. The former holds the source while being formed; the latter holds a substitute and examines a certain point in it. The former is concise, sharp, genuine, and direct, while the latter is long and adapted. The former examines the contrasts within it from a unified perspective, while the latter tries to sharpen the contrasts and turn the story into an ideological negotiation. The former stems from the direct link between the creation and its Israeli source, and the latter looks upon isssues from the reality of exile.

When reading the Israeli *aggadah* as it is expressed in the Jerusalem Talmud, says Zilka, we are astonished by its relevance to our present existence, as if two thousand years of exile do not separate us from it. Reading it, we return to the same soil, the same beloved places, the same essences of sacredness, the same land-dependent commandments, such as the *shmita* or sabbatical year, such as the prayers for rain, the same selfless devotion and sacrifice, the tangible yearning for the construction of the Temple. We return to the same land and it returns to us, wishing us to reveal in it again the true song of God, the song that cannot be sung on a foreign soil, and only through our return to the Torah of Israel will our return to our soil be complete.

The return to the Jerusalem Talmud is not an easy mission, says Zilka. This is not an edited and interpreted book; this is a genuine work of salvation of the Israeli Torah — the Torah that was abandoned in a corner. We should re-adopt it, understand its language and ways of thought, and revise and reinterpret it, not using known external tools for this purpose, but carving new ones out of its own manner of thought. If we listen to it directly and hear its singular voice, we will understand its unique tune.

THE UNIQUE CHARACTERISTICS
OF THE JERUSALEM TALMUD

Rabbi Avraham Hacohen Blas finds a variety of differences between the Jerusalem Talmud and the Babylonian Talmud: Why does only the Jerusalem Talmud say that every generation in whose time the Temple was not constructed is considered as if it has destroyed it? Why, according to the Jerusalem, is it that only he who deals with public needs is exempt from prayer? Why only in the Jerusalem does it say that a man who has neither learned, nor taught, nor has observed, nor carried out, and yet despite the fact that he was poor kept an institution for the study of Torah, receives a maximal mark of excellence from the Divine Court? Why, according to the Jerusalem, is lying permitted in order to bring Jews to Israel? And there are other examples. He answers: the Jerusalem Talmud tries to illuminate the Torah and convey it in the highest possible way and strengthen in its light the people's social, ethical, and national outlook.

The Israeli Torah—and its interpretation in the Jerusalem Talmud—is the Torah of the national revival, the foundation of Rabbi Kook's school.

The Jerusalem Talmud is concerned with values such as modesty (*anava*), as is illustrated by the following story: The People of Israel asked Honi Ha-Me'agel to pray for rain. Honi prayed, but no rain came down. The second time, Honi addressed God and told him that the People of Israel asked him to pray for rain, and this time the rains came. The Jerusalem wonders why it was that rain did not fall after the first prayer, and it answers that it was because of Honi's immodesty, since only the second time did he define himself as the public messenger whereas the first time he expected God to answer his prayer on account of his own good deeds.

Another example is what is said by the Jerusalem about King David (*Ta'aniyot 2: 9*): his sin was arrogance, because by counting the people, thus turning them into a compilation of individuals, he proved that he belittles them, whereas he should have understood that a king is a public delegate and his role is to uplift the public. However, in a wider examination, the Jerusalem sees in King David the model of the right leader, who had many achievements but still remained modest.

King Solomon too has failed with the same sin of arrogance, having told God that he built Him a temple, when he should have said that the people built it, not King Solomon alone.

The *Egla Arufa* story ("Beheaded female calf") presents one of the disputes between the two Talmuds: The Torah says that the town elders say that they did not kill this certain man, and the Talmud asks: Is it possible that the *Rabanim* are murderers? And the answer is: If the Court did not fulfill its duty, they are indeed as good as murderers. What is that duty? Here is where the dispute is seen: The Babylonian sages claim that the Court (the town elders) must act as a welfare society for every one in need, that is, care for his food, drink, and funeral, and if the town elders knew the victim and neglected him, it is possible that he died as a result of their neglect. Against this, the Israeli scholars claim that the Court's main role is to ascertain a fitting deterrence and to duly punish the criminals and not mitigate their punishment, because if they do, the deterrence factor is lost and the judges are considered as killers. The outlook of the Israeli sages is more general; they maintain that a fitting deterrence is needed rather than a specific concern.

Another example of the differences of opinion between the two Talmuds: Before the conquest of Jericho, Joshua ordered Israel, at his own initiative, not to loot. Did he act correctly? The Babylonian Talmud (*Sanhedrin* 44a, b) attacks his decision, explaining that God, by telling him to go (Joshua 7:11), accuses him of the Israeli defeat in the city of Ai. The Jerusalem Talmud, on the other hand, unambiguously states that Joshua was right in his decision; Jericho is banned and therefore it is forbidden to plunder it.

THE JERUSALEM WITHIN THE BABYLONIAN

During the *amoraim* period, the *nachoti* would convey issues and opinions between the academies of Israel and Babylonia, so that the teaching of both centers was known in both countries despite the tension between them. The issues in the Jerusalem Talmud were introduced in the Babylonian Talmud in their original shape and served as a basis for study by the Babylonian scholars. Conversely, in the Jerusalem Talmud, Babylonian issues appear alongside the Jerusalem ones. It is therefore possible to speak of the Jerusalem within the Babylonian and vice versa.

However, in other ways the Jerusalem and Babylonian Talmuds were not acquainted with each other, because in the Jerusalem Talmud there are Babylonian sayings that do not appear in the Babylonian Talmud. In addition, there are different versions of opinions that were delivered by the *nachoti* in Babylonia and that the Babylonian Talmud does not take into consideration. There are doubts that were discussed in the Babylonian Talmud and explained in the Jerusalem Talmud. Some of the mutual opinions which were explicitly brought in by both Talmuds are not included in the Talmud of their country of origin. Some of them are included in a different language and some contradict each other. There are elements that belong to a certain Talmud of a certain period—and do not appear later. There are also changes to the scholars' names as well as contradictions in versions of the outside opinions and the epigrams of the *amoraim* up to the last ones.

Therefore the editors of the Babylonian Talmud knew a former (or later) edition of a Jerusalem Talmud, which was given to them orally—or a Talmud of a different yeshiva.

Both Talmuds, as we have them today, disagree over the *halakhah* in several matters. On some issues, their *halakhah* was decided in opposing ways. Sometimes problems have remained in the Babylonian Talmud and are resolved in the Jerusalem Talmud. Some *halakhot* appear only in the Jerusalem Talmud, and some only in the Babylonian. For example: the *Bechorim* (firstborn) Fast on Passover Eve is mentioned in the Jerusalem Talmud (*Pesachim* 10:1; and also in *massekhet Sofrim*), but not in the Babylonian Talmud. On the other hand, there is no mention in the Jerusalem Talmud of Rabbah's words concerning prohibitions relating to the agricultural aspects of observing Succot, such as forbidding the reading of the *Megillah* (the book of Esther), or blessing the *lulav* (palm), or blowing the *shofar* (ram's horn) on Shabbat (*Pesachim* 9). In the Babylonian Talmud there are also terms and methods in the *halakhah* that do not appear at all in the Jerusalem Talmud.

· 9 ·

ATTITUDES TOWARD MEN AND
WOMEN IN THE TALMUD

IN HIS BOOK *Carnal Israel* (University of California Press, 1995), Daniel Boyarin speaks about the myth of manhood in Jewish society during the period of the Babylonian Talmud; that society preferred the intellectual perspective—the qualities of intellectual profundity and argumentation—over masculine power and admiration of muscle and sports, as worshipped by the Greeks, for example. Thus they placed the Torah and the house of study, the Bet Midrash, in the center of their world, rather than the Land of Israel, the territory itself, and the earth and the commandments related to the Holy Land. They focused on debates of all kinds, completely ignoring the subject of the Land of Israel. This attitude was a demonstration of machismo by the great *halakhah* elders who preferred the spirit to the soil in the form of the Land of Israel and the commandments related to the land.

The manhood motif is also prominent in different attitudes toward women and the relations between mothers and sons in the Babylonian Talmud versus the view in the Jerusalem Talmud.

Professor Shulamit Valer ("Women and Femininity in the Talmud Chapters," Hakibbutz Hameuchad Publication, 1993) claims that the Babylonian Talmud demonstrates strange relations between Rabbi Assi and his mother as they appear in the *Kiddushin* tractate. The old mother asks him for jewels and demands that he find her a husband as handsome as he is. His response is to escape Babylonia, where she lives, and go to the Land of Israel. The mother goes after him. Rabbi Assi asks permission to go welcome his mother and he vacillates between the answers of Rabbi Elazar, who denied his request, and Rabbi Johanan. Thus the mother died before he left to welcome her, and instead her coffin arrived.

The story of Rabbi Assi appears in the Jerusalem Talmud in three places: in the *Berachot* tractate (3a), the *Shvuot* tractate (6b), and the *Nazir* tractate (7a). In all these stories the conflict is whether the commandment of honoring our parents justifies leaving the Land of Israel and going to an impure land.

The Babylonian Talmud uses the core Israeli story and adds another story that changes its interest and its lesson. It does not find tenderness and delight in the decisions made by Rabbi Assi: He runs away from his mother, who stifles him with her fancies, and here the mother's arms "got longer" and she goes after him to the Land of Israel. Rabbi Assi does not intend to honor her, but rather he thinks that if he goes to welcome her, he can prevent her from settling next to him in the Land of Israel and thus he might be released from her madness. According to the Babylonian Talmud, Rabbi Yochanan doesn't know why Rabbi Assi wants to leave the Land of Israel, and he finds out only after he gives a negative answer to Rabbi Assi's request. Rabbi Assi asks the question: "Is it really?" meaning, is there no issue of honoring thy parents at all? Rabbi Assi's desire is merely to avoid his mother.

On the other hand, the Jerusalem Talmud and other Israeli sources explain that Rabbi Yochanan knew that Rabbi Assi wanted to go welcome his mother, either to assist her in entering the Land of Israel or to treat her with a warm welcome. The reference point is of empathy to the mother despite her strangeness. According to the Jerusalem Talmud, Rabbi Yochanan responds, "If you are certain you should go—go in peace," while the Babylonian Talmud says, "If you want to go, God will safely bring you back." Thus some people explain the situation by saying that Rabbi Yochanan feared that Rabbi Assi wanted to go back to Babylonia, that is, "bring you back" to Babylonia, the place fit for him. This interpretation implies that Rabbi Assi regretted coming to the Land of Israel and wanted to go back to Babylonia.

Rabbi Assi also expresses his sorrow that he went unnecessarily to the Land of Israel, according to the Babylonian Talmud: "If I only knew that my mother's death was so close, before I went, I would not need to escape and go to the Land of Israel."

According to the Jerusalem Talmud, Rabbi Assi became attached to Israel after he went there to avoid treating his mother with disrespect, and when he saw that she came after him, he went lovingly and respectfully to welcome her to the Land of Israel. All is more tender, gentle, and thoughtful and this reading shows us that his stay in the Land of Israel was not merely a matter of necessity and suffering.

The comparison of the stories about the ways of the mother (and a similar story of Rabbi Tarfon) also demonstrates the differences between the Babylonian Talmud and the Jerusalem Talmud. The mutual empathy between the mother and her son as it appears in the Jerusalem Talmud becomes a story that expresses the mother's domination of her son. She pressures him and uses him. The old and helpless mother needs her son only in the physical sense, and she dominates her submissive son by the power of her weakness. In general, the Babylonian Talmud demonstrates a harsher position toward the female gender.

The Jewish women of the Mishnah and Talmud period were isolated from the society and completely dependent on men. Some women took part in public life as equals and gained a respected independent status both in the business sector and in the elders' society. There were women whose expertise in various professional fields was no less than that of their male colleagues, who recognized their ability and their knowledge. However many women were considered a source of evil.

Over the generations, there were positive and negative attitudes toward the strictly kept separation of genders, even though socialization and friendships between men and women were not rare at all, either in the Israeli or in the Babylonian Jewish society, according to Professor Valer ("Women in the Jewish Society During the Mishnah and Talmud Period," Hakibbutz Hameuchad Publication, 2000).

One attitude finds its expression in the Babylonian Talmud essay (*Kiddushin* 80b): "Since the women are light-headed." The expression "light-headed women" also occurs elsewhere in the Talmud literature. In the Babylonian Talmud, *Shabbat* tractate (33b), this expression appears when Simeon bar Yohai explains to his son why they need to escape from their usual house of study and find a new hiding place. Rabbi Simeon's wife used to bring food daily to the hall where her son and husband studied. Rabbi Simeon feared that if the Romans discovered her, they would torture her, and she would be caught in her grief, in the sense of being unable to resist the powerful people and endure the torture (it may also mean rape).

Rashi adds a hard attitude of his own: Rashi interprets the prohibition of men to be alone with two women with the words: "Since they are light-headed and easy to be seduced and one should not be afraid of the other that might do the same." This is interpreted to mean that the reason the Mishnah prohibits a man from having sex with two women is fear of the women's impulses, while the reason for allowing a woman to be alone with two men is the moral strength of the men.

The hero of the story is the Babylonian Talmudic interpreter Rabbi Kahana as related in the Talmud (*Kiddushim* 39b).

> *Rabbi Kahana was selling straw baskets*
> *Claimed by that woman [for sex],*

And he answered her: I go and decorate myself.
He went up and fell from the roof to the ground.
Eliyahu came and accepted him [and got him].
He said to him: You bothered us for a great distance.
The man answered: Who caused that if not poverty?
So, he gave him a jar full of money.

Rabbi Kahana does not attempt to argue with the woman. He, like other story heroes presented in the Talmud, uses a trick to save himself from the destructive power of the woman. However, he does not try to stop her but rather jumps to his death, which is, in his opinion, the only way to be saved from sin. Rabbi Kahana's jump calls Eliyahu from a great distance, and he comes to save him.

In this story both the escape from the sin and the saving act are described in an extreme mode: there are no interim steps in the behavior of the escaping person, nor in the behavior of the woman who causes the sin. It seems that the author wants to say that the stronger the person's determination to escape from the sin, the more wonderful will be the saving act and even greater will be the prize.

All of these are lessons on how necessary it is to beware the woman and her seduction.

The Talmuds also demonstrate a difference in their judgment of men. The sacrifice involved in the mitzvah of living in the Land of Israel and its priority over the Diaspora is exemplified in the issue of "a good-looking captive woman" (Deut. 21:11–13):

11: and seest among the captives a beautiful woman, and
has a desire unto her, that thou wouldest have her to thy
wife;

12: then thou shalt bring her home to thine house; and she shall shave her head, and pare her nails;

13: and she shall put the raiment of her captivity from off her, and shall remain in thine house, and bewail her father and her mother a full month: and after that thou shalt go in unto her, and be her husband, and she shall be thy wife.

The Jerusalem Talmud says: you cannot have sexual intercourse with her until she has done all the listed actions. In contrast, the Babylonian Talmud permits intercourse with a good-looking woman during combat, which the Jerusalem Talmud strictly forbids, allowing it only after a month during which time she has made all the efforts to make her captor reject her; if he still wants her after that, he can have her.

The basic dichotomy here is between the Babylonian attitude, which is to guard man from himself, and the Jerusalem attitude, which is that man has the power to direct himself. The Babylonian claims that man is weak, and even if a beautiful woman is denied him, he will have her anyway, so it is preferable to permit it, as opposed to the Jerusalem, which expresses a deep belief in human power. It claims that although a beautiful captive may be in his hands, a man can still overcome his sexual drive during combat and also for a long time after it; a man has immense mental powers and we believe in him.

· 10 ·

THE TALMUD IN THE DIASPORA

THE INTERPRETATION OF THE TALMUD

Copies of the Talmud or single tractates from it reached the entire Diaspora. In the period before the destruction of the Second Temple, Jewish settlements already existed in many places in Asia, Africa, and Europe. However, from its beginning, the study of the Talmud was not an easy matter, even to scholarly students. Since the book is not edited in a systematic and orderly fashion, every single paragraph in it requires some measure of preliminary knowledge and not everyone would know the bases upon which every idea and issue were built.

The Talmudic material is also the fruit of the reflection of a living reality and of the research and debates in the institutions of religious study in Babylonia. Therefore readers from other countries and periods find it to be disconnected and not easy to comprehend. Indeed, in order to understand it, there is a need to complete sentences and ideas. Even its language aroused difficulties. The Aramaic-Hebrew jargon in which it was written was the spoken language of the Babylonian Jews for many generations. However, the Jews spoke the local languages of the countries they were living in as well, and even in Babylonia the Aramaic yielded to the Arabic language, which arrived there with the Moslem conquest in the mid-seventh century.

Thus it was difficult to study the Talmud in the Diaspora. The students needed explanations and commentary and they naturally turned to the heads of the larger yeshivas in Babylonia, Sura, and Pumbedita. The heads were respectfully called *geonim* (singular: *gaon*), which means genius. The title was shorthand for *Rosh Yeshivat Gaon Ya'akov* (Head of the yeshiva the brilliant Ya'akov), which initially was the title of the head of one of the larger yeshivas. After hundreds of years, the meaning of *geonim* changed and became the title of the scholars who followed the *amoraim* and who therefore were a primary source for understanding the Talmud.

The *geonim* continued teaching the Talmud according to the *amoraic* tradition and at times had a large number of students; however, they are remembered by their questions and responses. The Jewish communities would send them questions, mainly practical but also theoretical ones, regarding the understanding of the Talmud. In their response letter, the *geonim* would explain difficult words, obscure expressions, and even complete issues which were hard to grasp. These responses were a critical interpretation of the Talmud even though they were done not in a systematic or a perfect way, but as answers to the problems presented. Only the last *geonim* began to explain entire tractates. These explanations were mainly glossaries. Most of the *geonim*'s literature dealt chiefly with legal rulings and with practical conclusions from the Talmudic study.

In the eleventh century, at the termination of the *geonim*'s period and the decline of the spiritual center in Babylonia, two other important Jewish centers existed in the Diaspora. One was in the Magrheb countries (the Moslem West)— Northern Africa and Spain—and the other was in Europe, mainly France, Germany, and Italy. These two centers, which were the seeds of the Sephardic and Ashkenazi Jewry, differed greatly from each other in many respects. The Spanish-African (Sephardic) center was culturally the continuation of the Babylonian Jewry, who, like the latter, was under the rule of the Moslem empire, spoke Arabic, was influenced by it, and held a tight and uninterrupted contact with the Babylonian *geonim*. Thousands of responses, letters, and books arrived in Northern Africa from Babylonia, guiding the local Jews in *halakhic* practical matters and in maintaining their Judaism.

In contrast, the Jewry of Western Europe was very much attached to the Land of Israel, maintaining contact through Greece and Italy. Many of the versions of their prayers as well as basic concepts and perceptions came to them from Israel. Another central difference between the Sephardic and Ashkenazi Jewry at the time was the fact that the former was living in a sophisticated Arabic society, which was at its intellectual peak with regard to philosophy, science, poetry, and language, while the European environment of the Ashkenazi Jewry still existed in the Dark Ages. However, the Jews were on a much higher cultural level than their neighbors and had to create their own spiritual life almost without any ready-made models from the distant institutions of the Torah. It is not surprising, therefore, that in the domain of the interpretation of the Talmud two parallel trends developed: the Sephardic and the Ashkenazi.

The Sephardic scholars tended, in the wake of the *geonim*, to be more systematic and general in their attitude to the sources without dwelling too much on details. Their first commentary on the Talmud was that of Rabenu Hananel ben Hushiel, from Kairouan in North Africa, and was extremely short, tending to summarize every issue and give its main contents. He also explained the difficult words or phrases when necessary. Another contemporary commentary on the Talmud was written by his countryman Rav Nisim Gaon, *Mafteach Manuley HaTalmud* ("The Key for the Talmud's Locks"), which was both the title of his work and the name by which he is known. This commentary is less consecutive than the former and only highlights selected issues. These two commentaries contain a huge amount of the *geonim*'s theories and interpretations.

The need to find conclusions in the *halakhah*, understand issues as whole units of meaning, and try to achieve a synthesis of the Talmudic material continued throughout later generations. Such commentaries/interpretations, called *shitot* (methods) of the great Sephardic scholars, included *Sefer ha-Halakhot* by Rabbi Isaac Alfasi in the eleventh century in which he composed a digest of the Talmud to facilitate study; *The Interpretation of the Mishnayot* by Maimonides in the twelfth century; and the commentaries on the Talmud by Rabbi Meir Abulafia and the Ramban (Nachmanides or Rabbi Moshe ben Nachman) in the thirteenth century or the Rashba (Rabbi Shlomo ben Aderet) in the fourteenth century.

The interpretative method of the communities in Western Europe was rather different. During the *geonim* period, Europe already had great scholars of the Torah. The most famous among them was Rabenu Gershom of Meinz, called "Meor Hagola" ("The Light of the Diaspora"). He too wrote a short interpretation of various tractates in the Talmud. However, the greatest interpreter was his pupil's pupil, Rabbi Shlomo Yitzhaki from Troyes in France, known as Rashi. He lived in the eleventh century, studied in yeshivas in Germany and France, and wrote several books of rulings. He sent responses to questions and composed some liturgical poems for the service, some of which remain in the prayerbook to this day. However, his greatest works were his interpretations of the Torah and his monumental interpretation of the Babylonian Talmud, a brilliant example of a perfect reading: each section of it opened a way to analysis until this day.

Between the Sephardic and the Ashkenazi methods, there also existed a transitional approach, which developed in the important Jewish center in Southern France. Spiritually and geographically, the region was located between the Sephardic and the Ashkenazi Jewry. Their delegated interpreter was Rabbi Shlomo ben Menachem, called "Hameiri," who wrote the book *Bet Habechira,* in which he integrated the literal and textual interpretation of the Ashkenazi scholars with the summaries of the *sugyot* (decisions after internal debate) and *halakhot* of the Sephardic school. Unfortunately, this center was destroyed with the expulsion of the Jews from France and was never replaced.

PERSECUTION AND THE CENSORSHIP OF THE TALMUD

The scholars saw in the Oral Torah (the Mishnah and the Talmud) the unique assets of the People of Israel. According to one of the interpretations, in the future the Gentile nations will claim that they are the People of Israel, but God will tell them, "Whoever has my Mishnah is the real People of Israel." In this statement and in others, scholars stressed the importance of the Oral Torah, which is the stronghold of Judaism and which was regarded as dangerous, especially by the Christians, who in the seventh and eighth centuries tried unsuccessfully to inhibit its study. When the Catholic Church began to root out its internal enemies and persecute them, it simultaneously began to examine the Jewish books, especially the Talmud, thanks to some converted Jews, who from time to time would conduct public debates with the scholars, knowing only too well the value of the Talmud in the eyes of the Jews. Some of them tried to find evidence of the verity of Christianity in the Talmud itself, but these attempts were unsuccessful.

Rabbi Moshe ben Nachman, who was once allowed to argue freely with a converted Jew (*meshumad*), said that if this argument was correct, the Talmud scholars themselves would have been obliged to convert to Christianity. The fact that they remained Jewish only proves the nonexistence of these ridiculous "proofs."

On the other hand, some rulers and heads of the Church in Europe were convinced that the Talmud contained *anti*-Christian material, and on the basis of accusations by various informants, they ordered anything that spoke ill of Christianity and Jesus Christ to be erased.

The persecution of the Talmud climaxed in Paris in 1240, when Pope Gregory IX gave an order to burn the Talmud books. Similar orders were issued several more times during the thirteenth century, and in the case of Pope Clement IV in 1264 thousands of Talmud books were burned. This was an extremely distressing event for the Jews, who saw the burning of the Talmud as a great national disaster. Rabbi Meir from Rothenberg wrote a lament on this disaster, *Sha'ali Srufa ba'Esh*, which is still recited on Tisha B'Av, the holiday that commemorates the destruction of the First and Second Temples in Jerusalem.

Not all the European countries issued decrees to annihilate the Talmud. In Iberia the policy was only to have the statements that offended Christianity erased. In one case, in 1509, the heretic Johannes Pfefferkorn (sometimes spelled Pfferkorn) tried to incite the Church authorities to burn the Talmud in the countries ruled by Carl V (Germany and France), but then a Christian scholar named Johann Reuchlin argued in favor of the Talmud, and his arguments were effective, although not everywhere.

PRINTING OF THE TALMUD

A Sephardic author collected many *aggadot* and explained them, and they were printed in Constantinopole in 1511 under the title *Agadot Ha-Talmud* (The Talmud *Aggadah*).

Rabbi Ya'acov ben Rabi Shlomo ben Haviv wrote two works, *Eyn Yaakov* and *Bet Yaacov*, in which he compiled all the *aggadot* and *midrashim* and stories and moralistic studies from the entire Six Orders of the Mishnah in the Babylonian Talmud; it included explanations by Rashi as well as Tosafot (commentaries made in the margins) plus additions in the Talmud with the innovations of the Ramban, the Rashba, and Haran. The work was printed first in Constantinople in 1511 and again in 1546 in Venice and several times after that with new explanations. The most complete and elegant edition was printed in Vilna in 1890. A proofreader for the Vilna Printing House told a strange story about Rabbi Binyamin Musafia, the author of *Musaf He'aruch*; he claimed that the rabbi composed an interpretation for the Jerusalem Talmud and left instructions in his will to have it buried with him in his grave.

Pope Leo X allowed the Talmud to be printed in 1520, but this period of grace was short lived. In 1553, following the strengthening of the counter-reformation movement, several informants caught the ear of Pope Julius III, who ordered the Talmud destroyed; tens of thousands of books were set afire. The pope's order prevented its printing in Italy but indirectly changed the history of printing throughout Europe. In many countries the printing of the Talmud required a permit from the authorities, and this could be obtained mainly by Christian printers. Eventually the censorship on Jewish holy books and in particular the Talmud became tighter.

In 1564 Pope Pius IV allowed the Talmud to be printed again on condition that the offending passages be erased. The censorship continued, and as a result even exemplary editions of the Talmud in our day are not complete, containing changes and additions made by the censor.

The Basel (Switzerland) Edition of the Talmud (1578 and

onward) is a very abridged edition, which even dropped the
tractate on idolatry *(Avodah Zarah)*, and unfortunately many
later editions were forced to be printed similarly.

· 11 ·

OPPOSITION TO THE TALMUD

*T*HE HISTORICAL ROOTS of opposition to the Talmud lie in the opposition to the Oral Law and to the authority of the scholars (*hachamim*).

As early as the Second Temple period (sixth century BCE), certain scholars renounced the main bulk of the Oral Law and claimed the interpretational authority to themselves; among them were the Sadducees and the Essenes. The Talmud hints at a collection of laws of various "heretic" sects and "externists," knowledge about whom was limited until the Dead Sea Scrolls were discovered.

There are also allusions to Judeo-Christian sects in the Talmud, but the term "heretics" is not always directed at

Christians, as was claimed by those unjustifiably accusing the Talmud of anti-Christian rhetoric. It is assumed that the remnants of these sects continued to exist; but during the Middle Ages (and later on) the main objection to the Talmud and to the Rabbinical Judaism dependent on it was on the part of the Karaites, who were strong in Babylonia, Egypt, and Israel.

The Karaites believed only in the word of the Scriptures— the five books of the Torah, the Prophets, and the Writings, collectively known as the *Tanakh*; interpretations such as those that were carried down in the Oral Law and written down in the Mishnah and the Talmud were rejected by them as the words of men rather than the Word of God.

Their active opposition evoked a lengthy and diversified conflict which produced a ramified literature for and against the Talmud. Rav Saadyah Gaon was among those mounting a forceful counterattack, and against this background Rav Sherira Gaon composed a letter on the history of the Talmud's literature. Famous Karaite compositions were written by Anan Ben David, Benjamin ben Moses Nahavendi, Daniel el-Kumasi, and others.

In the middle of the seventeenth century, against the background of a Marrano-Christian issue (Marranos, a pejorative term, also called Conversos, were forcibly converted Jews who secretly practiced Judaism), there were some small elements of resistance to the Talmud and the *halakhah* in Amsterdam on the part of Uriel d'Acosta, Baruch Spinoza, and others.

The beginning of the Frankist group in Poland in the middle of the eighteenth century, also named "The Talmud Opposers" (the group eventually converted to Christianity), is rooted in the aftermath of the messianic movement of Shabtai Zvi, whose followers rejected the Talmud altogether and replaced it with the Book of Zohar and the Kabbalah.

In the New Age (eighteenth century), most of the Haskalah (enlightenment) movements, including the Reform movement, exhibited opposition to the Talmud, since they saw in it a chief impediment to the accomplishment of their social and religious goals. The scholars of these movements often attacked the Talmud in writing, claiming that it was outdated, based on mistakes and superstitions, abounding with disputes and internal contradictions, disorderly and confusingly edited, and so on. For a while the dispute on this issue became a central motif in the Haskalah literature and in some measure also in the renewing *Hochmat Israel* (wisdom of the Jewish people).

"MY POWER AND THE MIGHT OF MINE HAND"

The renewal of the Jewish settlement in the Land of Israel in the twentieth century, and furthermore the existence of the State of Israel, have brought up again the need to use force (excluding, of course, the armed rebellion in the ghettos during the Holocaust). The establishment of the state in a place that was, in contrast to the false slogan attributed to Lord Balfour—"A land without a People to a People without a land"—partly settled by another people, has created a situation of national conflict that has developed through the years into an ongoing violent conflict.

In this context it is interesting to note that the Orthodox rabbinical world was opposed to the Zionist movement and to the establishment of the State of Israel before the arrival of the Messiah, and the most poignant formulation of this concept was written by the Rabbi of Satmar, Rabbi Yoel Teitle-baum, mainly in his book *Ve Yoel Moshe* (*And Moses Swore*) as well as in a composition he published after the Six-Day War called "On the Redemption and the Recompense."

In his writings, and mainly in *Ve Yoel Moshe*, the Rabbi of Satmar expressed his vehement opposition to Zionism on the "Three Vows" midrash, in which he sees a *halakhic* guidance that negates a struggle for the establishment of a Jewish state.

The midrash is based on three verses appearing in *Shir HaShirim* (The Song of Solomon 2:7):

> *I charge you, O ye daughters of Jerusalem, by the roes, and by the hinds of the field, that ye stir not up, nor awake my love, till he please.*

> *I charge you, O daughters of Jerusalem, that ye stir not up, nor awake my love, until he please.*

> *I charge you, O ye daughters of Jerusalem, by the roes, and by the hinds of the field, that ye stir not up, nor awake my love, till he please.*

The midrash of these verses is based on the traditional interpretation of The Song of Solomon, according to which this book is an allegory of the relations of God and the Jews:

> *"These three vows, why?" One—that Israel will vow not to climb up the wall, and two—that God made Israel vow not to rebel against the world's nations, and three—that God made the pagans vow not to be too subjected to Israel.* (*Babylonian Ketuvot* 111a).

Rabbis and religious scholars who support Zionism, or at least did not oppose it theologically, coped with the theological arguments of the Rabbi of Satmar in various ways. Some saw in this an *aggadic* essay without a *halakhic* validity. Others argued that the vows had been annulled since the world's nations have breached them as well. Also there were rabbis who interpreted "not to climb on the wall" as the construction of the Temple rather than the mass *aliyah* (immigration) and the establishment of a state.

There was also a movement called "Brith Shalom," which was created in 1925 by a group of Jewish intellectuals who wished to establish peaceful co-existence between Jews and Arabs by giving up the right to build a national home for the Jews in Israel as put forth in the Balfour Declaration. This movement proposed the formation of a bi-national autonomy under the British Mandate in which Arabs and Jews would enjoy complete political and civil equality.

Among the friends and supporters of this movement were Arthur Rupin, the philosopher Martin Buber, the philosopher Shmuel Hugo Bergman, the Kabbalah researcher Gershom Scholem, the educator Ernst Simon, and the first president of Hebrew University Yehuda Leib Magnes. Additional supporters were the businessman Shlomo Zalman Schocken and the British statesman Herbert Samuel. The movement was reduced to a marginal factor in Zionism after the majority of the Jewish Congress rejected its views and aspired to establish a sovereign Jewish state free of the British Mandate. The Arabs too did not display readiness to cooperate with this faction. In August 1930 it was dismantled.

In Deuteronomy (8:7–20) Moses points to a problem:

> God brings you into a good land "a land of wheat and barley.… A land wherein thou shalt eat bread without scarceness… thou shalt not lack any thing in it";

And out of this abundance:

"Beware that thou forget not the LORD thy God, in not keeping his commandments, and his judgments, and his statutes:

12: Lest when thou hast eaten and art full,

14: Then thine heart be lifted up, and thou forget the LORD thy God, which brought thee forth out of the land of Egypt, from the house of bondage;

And then:

17: And thou say in thine heart, My power and the might of mine hand hath gotten me this wealth.

Because if you forget:

19: And it shall be, if thou do at all forget the LORD thy God, and walk after other gods, and serve them, and worship them, I testify against you this day that ye shall surely perish.

20: As the nations which the LORD destroyeth before your face, so shall ye perish; because ye would not be obedient unto the voice of the LORD your God.

This strong statement identifies the attitude of *kochi ve-ozem yadi* with "you have forgotten your God" and this attitude brings the People of Israel to ruin and their fate will not be different from that of the pagan natives.

Further on Moses points out an additional danger liable to occur to the People upon entering to the Land (Deut. 9:4–5):

4: Speak not thou in thine heart, after that the LORD thy God hath cast them out from before thee, saying, For my righteousness the LORD hath brought me in to possess this land:

but for the wickedness of these nations the LORD doth drive them out from before thee.

*5: **Not for thy righteousness**, or for the uprightness of thine heart, dost thou go to possess their land: **but for the wickedness of these nations** the LORD thy God doth drive them out from before thee, **and that he may perform the word which the LORD** swore unto thy fathers, Abraham, Isaac, and Jacob."*

The People of Israel, who are entering the Promised Land when other peoples have been deported from it because of their sins, may delude themselves and think: This will not happen to us because we are better than they are. In the above verses Moses warns the People of Israel: This delusion is dangerous; you are not better people; the natives were deported because of their deeds; this land was given to you because God made a covenant with the Avot—the Fathers. However, Israel is a land where "the eyes of the Lord thy God are within it," and it is sensitive to the behavior of its inhabitants and throws out the sinners. And if you behave the way your predecessors did, your fate will be identical to theirs.

· 12 ·

WHAT BECAME OF THE JERUSALEM TALMUD?

$\mathcal{W}$E KNOW NEXT to nothing about the spread of Torah study in Israel after the completion of the Jerusalem Talmud. The *halakhah* and *aggadah* creation had not stopped, and the Babylonian scholars known as *savoraim* continued to send questions to the scholars of Israel. However, the Babylonians were concerned with their own Talmud and dedicated their energy to its explanation and spread. In 747 CE, with the rise of the Abbasid Caliphate, Babylonia and its capital Baghdad became the center of the Arabic world, a fact that helped the Babylonian *geonim* (heads of the yeshivas in Sura and Pumbedita) to establish their Talmud as the dominant one. As a result, the study of the Jerusalem Talmud became the territory of the individual. The first *geonim* hardly knew it at all, and those who did looked at it only to see the verses on prayers.

Beginning with Rav Saadyah Gaon, this situation changed. He was born in Egypt, where communities of people from Israel lived, and he also lived in Israel himself for a while. He explicitly mentions the Jerusalem Talmud in one of his responses and uses it to explain the Torah as well as in his philosophical work *Emunot ve-De'ot* ("Faiths and Opinions").

The Jerusalem Talmud was known to those who assembled the Babylonian. The first of the *geonim* who quotes the Jerusalem version is Rav Saadyah, who called it "Talmud Israel." Rabenu Nisim in Kairouan (Northern Africa) worked with it frequently. And the Sephardic or Spanish scholars worked with both Talmuds and only in cases of disagreements between the two did they give priority to the Babylonian.

In France the Jerusalem Talmud was not known at first, and even the famed French rabbi Rashi did not see it. However, he copied some matters from it that he found in other books. In the period of post-Rashi scholars, the Jerusalem Talmud was quoted many times. The first legal interpreters (*poskim*) used the Jerusalem often, so they probably had an entire copy of it, as we have it today or perhaps in some smaller forms. The late *poskim* stopped referring to the Jerusalem Talmud and dealt only with the Babylonian. The study of the Jerusalem Talmud was less common, perhaps because of the absence of a Rashi interpretation for it and because of its language—Sursi or Persian Hebrew—which is more difficult than the Babylonian language.

A center for the distribution of the Jerusalem Talmud was in Kairouan, which is in contemporary Tunisia. In a book called *Metivot*, which was probably written in the tenth century, a "Jerusalem Version" was given as a parallel and complement to the Babylonian Talmud's *halakhot*. In the eleventh century, Rav Nisim Gaon used it to explain several obscurities in the Babylonian Talmud, and Rabenu Hananel adjoined it to the Babylonian Talmud in his explanation of the latter.

The Jerusalem Talmud arrived in Spain from Kairouan. It was first explicitly mentioned by Rabbi Shmuel Hanagid and later in the eleventh century by Rabbi Yitzhak ben Giat, who used it frequently.

Maimonides referred to the Jerusalem Talmud in his explanation of the Mishnah and in his book *Mishne Torah*, especially in the book *Zraim*, and at times he even ruled according to it in contrast to the Babylonian Talmud. Maimonides also composed a special work titled *Hilchot Ha-yerushalmi* (The Laws of the Jerusalem Talmud), thus restoring the splendor of the Jerusalem Talmud to its earlier status.

The Ramban (Nachmanides) used the Jerusalem Talmud extensively to interpret the Babylonian Talmud and at the same time explained its language.

In addition some scholars in Provence used it.

After the Expulsion from Spain in 1492 and the immigration to Israel, Israeli scholars began to use it, mainly the Order on Seeds (*seder Zeraim*) to establish the observation of the land-dependent commandments. One of them, Rabbi Shlomo Sirilyo, composed one of best short and straight explanations on the Order on Seeds, as well as a passage on money and value (*massekhet Shekalim*).

From the eighteenth century onward the study of the Jerusalem Talmud in Ashkenaz (Germany) increased. The first important commentator was Rabbi Eliyahu Fulda, who wrote commentary on *seder* (Order) *Zeraim* and *massekhet* (tractate) *Shekalim* and was very influential. In the next generation two great Jerusalem Talmud scholars wrote commentaries on the *seder Nashim* (laws pertaining to women and family life) and *seder Moed* (laws concerning festivals and fasts) as well as a few more passages.

THE MANUSCRIPTS

Notwithstanding the efforts of those who would destroy the Talmud, in the sixteenth century, when the Jerusalem Talmud was printed in Venice, there were several manuscripts. Rabbi Isaschar Ber Ben Naphtali mentions a good and handsome Jerusalem Talmud on a very old parchment and so do other rabbis. Rabbi Yosef Kurkus mentions a "proof read Jerusalem," Rabbi Hayyim Joseph David Azulai (the Hida) saw Rabbi Menachem's proofs of the Jerusalem Talmud, and there was another which was proofread by Rabbi Bezalel Ashkenazi. However, all these were lost. Today we have only the following:

The **Leiden Manuscript** is the only one containing the entire Jerusalem Talmud. It is written by Rabbi Yechiel Anu, who completed writing the *Zeraim* and *Moed* Orders on the 12th of Shevat (1289), and the *Nashim* and *Nezikin* Orders six weeks later. He also added corrections, completions, and other versions, on the sheet and between the lines. Every chapter's mishnah is written preceding the *gemara*, and short paragraphs are repeated before each *halakhah*; in the tractate on *Berachot*, the mishnah is integrated in its entirety within the Gemara. This manuscript was proofread and prepared for printing by the Venetian printers according to their evidence, matching with three other copies of the Jerusalem Talmud.

The **Rome Manuscript**, held at the Vatican (33), contains the *seder Zeraim*, excluding the tractate *Bikurim* (First Fruits), and the tractate *Sota* (Adultress) from *seder Nashim* and was probably written in the thirteenth century. It is full of mistakes and large omissions, but it contains original versions, and in many places it fills out the deficiencies of the Leiden manuscript.

"**The Jerusalem's Remains**" is the large compilation of sections of the Jerusalem Talmud which was recovered from the *geniza* or storeroom of an old synagogue in Cairo, Egypt, and published by L. Ginzburg in New York in the Hebrew year Tarsat (1908–1909).

The **Sephardic Manuscript** is an almost complete copy of *massekhet Nezikin* of the Jerusalem Talmud and was discovered by Shmuel Rosenthal among the photocopies or Hebrew manuscripts in the National and University Library in Jerusalem. It was thought to be written in the middle of the fifteenth century and is considered a good manuscript from the point of view of the versions of the Jerusalem Talmud as well as of its Jerusalem language—both the Hebrew and the Galillean-Aramaic—concerning the originality of its spelling and pronunciation.

THE FORGERY OF THE JERUSALEM TALMUD

Early in the twentieth century, Rabbi Shlomo Yehuda Friedlaender published several sections of the Jerusalem Talmud—the Order *Kiddushin* (Holy Things), *massekhet Khulin*, and *massekhet Bechorot* in the Hebrew year Tarsaz (1906–1907) as well as *massekhet Zevachim* and *massekhet Arachin*, (Tarsat)—however, their author eventually acknowledged that they were a forgery.

According to the detailed story behind the forgery,

Friedlaender announced that he had found a unique and "extremely old" manuscript of *seder Kiddushin* (the Order of laws relating to the sanctuary and food) of the Jerusalem Talmud and had already printed from it the following passages: *Zevachim, Arachin, Khulin,* and *Bechorot.* He said that his brother, who traded in the town of Izmir and its surroundings, bought old books from the legacy left by Rabbi Yehoshua Benvenisti, the author of *Sdei Yehoshua,* on the Jerusalem Talmud (Six Orders of the Mishnah), and among these books was the above-mentioned manuscript, which was given to Yehoshua Benveniste by Don Avraham Halevi, one of the Portuguese Marranos who returned to Judaism in Kushta (current-day Istanbul), and who got it from the priest previously known as Don Shlomo Narbono of Barcelona.

This manuscript contained Gemara of the Westerners (*Gemara di'vney Ma'arava,* meaning Israel, as opposed to Babylonia in the East) that includes the entire *seder Nezikin* and *seder Kiddushin* as well as the tractate *Temurah.* This manuscript came into the possession of the wealthy Suleiman Benvenest, who used it as a talisman. In 1902 Friedlaender obtained it on loan and with great difficulty succeeded in copying it. The author's name appears in the manuscript as follows:

> *"I, the writer, Yitzhak bar Yoseph Ilbergluni, wrote all the Jerusalem Talmud as far as here, and with the help of God I shall complete it, for the Chacham [Wise man], a Minister in Israel, Don Yitzhak Halevi, who spent much gold to decorate and glorify it in honor of the Great Creator, Blessed be His Name, etc., and I have copied it from accurate books and terms in the same version as they were copied by Mar Avi N.B.M. from the Jerusalem, which was controlled by Rabenu*

*Hai Gaon—Rosh Hagola, and the work was completed on
25 Tamuz of the year 4972 (1312 ce). And the manuscript of
the tractates Khulin and Temurah were written by the writer
Yitzhak Farhi of Kushta (Istanbul) (in 1670)."*

However, when this Jerusalem Talmud was published,
it was rejected by some important rabbis, who claimed it to
be a forgery, or at the most a compilation of essays which
already existed in the Jerusalem Talmud in other tractates.
Refutation came from the well-regarded rabbi Dr. Ritter
from Amsterdam, as well as others. They proclaimed that
it certainly wasn't the original Jerusalem Talmud. Others,
however, said that it was a compilation of existing compositions on other tractates by a single writer (whether an early
or a late one), and one thought that this was the *gemara* for
the tractate *Kelim* composed by two *amoraim*, Rabina and
Rav Ashi.

This volume of *massekhet Minkhot* and *massekhet Temurah*
was never printed. Some years ago a manuscript was brought
to Israel containing *massekhet Minkhot* and *massekhet Temurah* (probably copied from Friedlaender's original copy), as
well as *massekhet Berachot* from the "Tanina Edition" of the
Jerusalem Talmud.

There is not a strong enough basis to assume the existence
of a Jerusalem version for *seder Tahorot.*

From the second half of the twentieth century there were
a great many photocopied editions of the Babylonian Talmud, most of them after the template of Vilna's print, but
some also in various sizes and forms. However, the inven-
tion of photography brought a standstill to further editing.
Solecisms and printing errors were thus eternalized, though
in various places and particularly in Israel attempts were

made to improve the Talmudic text, adding to it punctuation signs, *nikkud* (diacritical marks), and some illustrations, and perhaps these will mark a new line of development. It is still awaiting its redeemer.

The ways of the construction and editing of the Jerusalem Talmud were similar to those of the Babylonian Talmud. It began with the *amoraim* attaching *baraitot* to the Mishnah, explaining it or opposing it. Later on they gradually added explanations and *halakhot* (verdicts) that they inferred from the Mishnah and the *baraitot*; *halakhot* that were not mentioned in the Mishnah, as well as new problems and deeds preceding them; and eventually the debates of the last *amoraim* on the words of their predecessors, their own innovations and the debate on them.

At times the Jerusalem's Mishnah differs from that of the Babylonian. For some single *mishnayot*, there is evidence that Rabbi Judah Ha-Nasi changed them or wrote them in two different versions and that the Jerusalem chose the first edition version.

The Jerusalem Talmud is a closed book for the Torah learners, though in recent years more people have turned to it, but the fact is that people are deterred by certain stigmas that have adhered to it. The first claim is that the Jerusalem's versions are incorrect, and since we have only a single consecutive manuscript, the Leiden Manuscript, which contains too many errors, it's untrustworthy. One cannot deny the fact that the Jerusalem Talmud contains many inaccuracies; however we should be grateful to the Academy for the Hebrew Language, which has published a corrected edition of the Leiden Manuscript reducing the number of errors.

The claim that the existing number of versions is a factor

that interrupts the proper understanding of the Jerusalem Talmud may be true with regard to the theoretical *halakhic* treatises; however, in the *aggadic* (legendary) tractates, even if there are minor errors, they don't disrupt the study of the Talmud.

Another claim is that the vocabulary and structure of the Aramaic language of the Jerusalem Talmud are different from those of the Babylonian. This is true, but it is not a completely different language. And learning a language is simply a matter of drilling. Torah students got accustomed to the Babylonian Talmud at an early age and therefore have no problem studying it. A mild effort can make us fluent in the Jerusalem Talmud's language fairly quickly. Current students of the Jerusalem Talmud do not recognize these differences as drawbacks; the style is easy and fluent, and those who have "walked in" do not experience any difficulty.

The Gaon from Poltova, Rabbi Yitzhak Isaac Krasilzikov, wrote in the introduction to his interpretation of the Jerusalem Talmud, *Toldot Yitzhak*, that those who are accustomed to studying the Jerusalem Talmud find its concise language and style appealing and "sweeter than honey," and find traces of our sages' language with its age-old grace.

The late Rabbi Yisachar Tamar wrote in his book *Aley Tamar:* "He who is used to the Jerusalem knows that its language is not enigmatic. This is its style: concise, accurate, and clear, and its main editing work is exemplary."

Fortunately, more and more popular interpretations are being published these days that help the student enter the Jerusalem's realm; its increasing study will improve our comprehension of many of its issues that were not understood until now.

PART THREE

· 13 ·

The Meaning of *Aliyah*
through the Generations

---

*W*HETHER IT WAS guilt for not following the biblical commandment to live in the Land of Israel or simply a love of the Holy Land and a yearning to absorb the spiritual comfort it could provide, over the centuries Jews from around the world undertook the often arduous journey to the Land of our Forefathers, realizing the mitzvah of making *aliyah*, of returning to Israel. Some settled there permanently. Others left after warming themselves by the fire of their faith. Still others intent upon coming were caught by pressing exigencies in their native lands and never completed the trip.

ALIYAH OF THE AMORAIM—THE TALMUD SAGES

As we have seen, following the destruction of the Second Temple, Babylonia became the spiritual center of the Jewish People, a center which was headed by the exilarch or Rosh Hagola, who organized and directed communal life and chiefly spiritual life. The yeshivas there flourished, producing the Babylonian Talmud. Nevertheless, during this period there was an *aliyah* to Israel of some of the *amoraim*. While we can assume that their *aliyah* ensued from a love of the Holy Land, there were other motivations as well, such as the desire to study the Torah with the famous sages of Israel. In addition, many came seeking a *semikhah*, the term for ordination, the granting of which was available only in Israel.

Two of the most outstanding sages making *aliyah* were Rabbi Yehuda Halevi and Maimonides (Rabbi Moses ben Maimon). Yehuda Halevi was an eminent scholar and poet, born in Toledo, Spain, in 1075. His chief work is *The Kuzari*, and his famous poems express the yearning to Zion, some of which were inserted into the Tisha B'Av laments, and urged *aliyah* to the Land of Israel along the generations.

Maimonides, the greatest scholar of his time, left Northern Africa and went to the Land of Israel in 1165. After several months he made his way to Jerusalem and later returned to Egypt, where he died. His body was brought to Tiberias for burial next to the tomb of Rabbi Yochanan ben Zakai, a first-century sage and *tanna* during the time of the Second Temple.

Maimonides in his epistles wrote that those who persuade themselves to stay in their place, saying they plan to study until the Messiah arrives in the Western countries and then they will go to Jerusalem, are committing an offense and causing the others to commit an offense.

One of the Bible's greatest interpreters, Nachmanides— who was born Moses (Moshe) ben Nachman, in Girona, Spain, in 1194—carried out his own preaching and arrived in Israel at the age of 73, at first in Akko (Acre) and later in Jerusalem. Unfortunately, he managed to live there only three years, during which time he completed an interpretation of the Torah and taught many students from Israel as well as from Babylonia. He is buried in Haifa.

An impressive *aliyah* took place in 1211 when three hundred rabbis from France and England came to the Land of Israel. Among them were Rabbi Yehonathan of Lonil, one of the great scholars of Provence, and Rabbi Shimon of Shantz, one of the important Baalei ha-Tosafot (commentators on the Talmud) of his generation. Against the background of the occupation of Jerusalem by Salah al-Din (Saladin) and its delivery from the Crusaders and from persecutions and religious decrees and economic difficulties, some of the rabbis settled in Jerusalem and some in Akko. Several years later, in 1258, another group arrived from France headed by Rabbi Yechiel of Paris who conducted the famous Paris Disputation (1240), in which he successfully defended Judaism in a debate with a convert, but which unfortunately brought about the burning of the Talmud there in 1244. He too settled in Akko and established a yeshiva there with three hundred students.

In 1360 some small groups and individuals arrived in Israel mainly from Spain, Italy, Germany, England, France, and northern Africa. The year 1391 was one of particularly heavy decrees in Spain, and more Jews and *Anusim* (Marranos/

Conversos) from there came to Israel. A larger wave of immigrants took place a century later during the expulsion from Spain (1492) and five years later from Portugal. The *aliyah* became denser with the Ottoman occupation of Palestine by the Turks in 1516. Newcomers moved into Jerusalem and its vicinity, but more settled in Safed and its surroundings, which had become the spiritual center of the country. Among its important scholars was Rabbi Yosef Karo, who in 1335 arrived in Safed, where he wrote his important *halachic* book *Shulhan Arukh*.

FROM THE MOSLEM COUNTRIES AND BEYOND

Jews began to arrive in Israel from the Moslem countries in the fifteenth century, coming from Northern Africa. At the end of the sixteenth century and the beginning of the seventeenth, some Jewish scholars from Morocco arrived in the Land of Israel and settled in Safed, where they became prominent.

From Izmir in Turkey in 1740 came Rabbi Chayim Abulafia, who was invited by the Ottoman ruler of the Galilee to reside in Tiberias.

In the nineteenth century the Yehuda family came from Bagdad, Iraq, and built Torah institutions and synagogues in Jerusalem. Another famous arrival was Rabbi Eliyahu Mani, who served as Hebron's chief rabbi and developed the community spiritually and economically.

Yemenite Jews began arriving in the eighteenth century, but it was only at the end of the nineteenth century, in 1882, that the mass *aliyah* began, based on the yearning for salvation. In addition, Yemen had been occupied by the Turks ten years earlier, a fact that strengthened the link with the

Holy Land. The 1882 *aliyah* was fraught with hardships—a cholera epidemic killed many of them en route. Convoys walked all the way from Zan'a to the port of Hudeida, from where they sailed in small boats to Alexandria and from there made their way to Jaffa.

From Bukhara and Georgia came Rabbi Efrayim Kukia, who in 1863 built a neighborhood called Ohel Avraham, near the Damascus Gate in Eastern Jerusalem. Sir Moshe Montefiore found two hundred Georgian Jews in Jerusalem and praised their bravery.

The first newcomer from Bukhara, Rabbi David Melamed Heifetz, arrived in 1821. In 1882 there was a large *aliyah* from there. In 1889 some wealthy Jews from Bukhara, Tashkent, and Samarkand arrived in Jerusalem and established a neighborhood of their own named "Rehovot." To this day it is called Rehovot Ha-Bukharim. Up until the Russian Revolution, the neighborhood was one of the richest in Jerusalem, thanks to its trade with the old country.

Many prominent scholars making *aliyah* in the sixteenth to eighteenth centuries were from Poland. The largest group, with fifteen hundred people, reached Jerusalem in 1700, headed by Rabbi Yehuda Hachasid, who bought a large courtyard and built a synagogue and a residential neighborhood as well. However, in 1721 the Moslems burned down the synagogue. Its ruins, called Hurvat Rabbi Yehuda Hachasid, still stand there today.

The *aliyah* of the pupils of the Baal Shem Tov (Israel ben Eliezer, founder of Hasidism) began with the 1747 *aliyah* of his brother-in-law, Rabbi Avraham from Kitov, who was the only Ashkenazi sage in the Bet El Yeshiva in Jerusalem.

In 1777 a large *aliyah* headed by the pupils of the Maggid

of Mezritch as well as other Hasidic leaders arrived from Lithuania. Rabbi Zalman of Lyady was supposed to arrive as well, but he decided midway to go back in order not to leave the Lithuanian Hasidim without a shepherd.

A special *aliyah* was that of Rabbi Nachman of Bratzlav, who at the age of 26 decided to come to Israel. He arrived in Haifa in 1798 and from there he moved to Tiberias and later to Safed. Among his famous sayings are: "Wherever I go I'm going to the Land of Israel." "Every view and thought I have are due only to my residence in the Land of Israel since the chief wisdom resides in the Land of Israel."

From Hungary came the Chatam Sofer pupils. He came to the conclusion that it was not possible to speed up salvation and only the settlement of the Land of Israel could bring it about; therefore he demanded that his pupils make *aliyah*. He also maintained that working the land in Israel was a mitzvah in itself.

RASHI ON THE "PRAISE OF ISRAEL"

Rashi (Rabbi Shlomo Yitzhaki, 1040–1145) interpreted the entire Holy Scriptures and it was said of him that he "improved" the Babylonian Talmud, since everyone could find his own wish in his interpretation, the small one according to his capacity and the big one according to his strength. His *Interpretation of the Torah* was the first book published in Hebrew in Italy, in 1475. Since then, his interpretation and the Holy Scriptures have become inseparable. To distinguish between his interpretation and the Torah writing, his interpretation was printed in lettering of a design based on the Judeo-Spanish writing and came to be known as "The Rashi Script," although Rashi had nothing to do with the printer's decision. Added to Rashi's own interpretation were close to fifty interpreters who tried to explain his words and ideas. He did not interpret the entire Talmud by himself; some of the items credited to him were composed by his grandchildren, who followed his unique interpretational way.

Although he never lived in Israel and admitted that he would have been more knowledgeable if he had, his many interpretations testify to his familiarity with the Holy Land which derived from his mastery in the Torah. He knew its geography in detail and even drew maps of Israel to illustrate the portion of the weekly Torah reading when it dealt with travel. He was consistent in his praise of Israel and never spoke ill of it. The following verses from Deuteronomy 11:10–12 that compare Israel to Egypt exemplify his fondness for Israel, though some scholars think otherwise:

> *10: For the land, whither thou goest in to possess it, is not as the land of Egypt, from whence ye came out, where thou sowedst thy seed, and wateredst it with thy foot, as a garden of herbs:*

> *11: But the land, whither ye go to possess it, is a land of hills and valleys, and drinketh water of the rain of heaven:*

> *12: A land which the LORD thy God careth for: the eyes of the LORD thy God are always upon it, from the beginning of the year even unto the end of the year.*

These verses are interpreted by him as saying that Israel, the land they are going to inherit, is not like Egypt but better.

HA-ARI HAKADOSH (THE HOLY ARI),
RABBI ISAAC LURIA

The great Hasidic scholars drew their love of Israel and the duty to settle there from the Kabbalah scholars, and especially from the Ashkenazi Rabbi Ari Isaac Luria "Ha-Ari" (the Lion), who was the greatest mystic of Safed in Israel in the sixteenth century, and who added a new and unique layer to the study of Jewish esoteric teachings. He was born in Jerusalem in 1534, and at the age of eight, after his father's death, he was taken by his mother to Egypt, where they lived with her wealthy brother, who cared for the boy as his son. At age fifteen he married his cousin and continued to study both the Torah (with Rabbi David ben Zimra, who was at that time the chief rabbi of Egypt) as well as Jewish mysticism. It is said that he spent the weekdays on his own in a house near the Nile River, where he studied the Book of Zohar, returning home for the weekend. He remained there until the prophet Eliyahu Hanavi was revealed to him, ordering him to go to Israel, settle in Safed, and teach the local Rabbi Chaim Vital whatever he knew, because interpreting Luria's teaching was to be Vital's life mission.

In 1570 the Ari arrived in Safed and for the next two years he taught the Kabbalah, Jewish mysticism, to Rabbi Vital and some other pupils. His Kabbalah system is used to this day.

The Ari saw himself as the ben Yoseph Messiah. On the Sabbath he would wear a white dress folded into four with the four-letter name of the Lord on it. He and his pupils would gather every Friday night and confess their sins and visit the tomb of Rabbi Simeon bar Yohai. He never actually wrote a book of his own, but his pupil Rabbi Chaim Vital wrote books which contain his mentor's teaching.

The Ari, as he appears in Vital's writings, talked a lot about Israel and its holiness. He said, for example, interpreting Deuteronomy 8:9, that "a land in which you will eat bread without scarcity, in which you will lack nothing" is a land where one lives not only on bread but also on every utterance of the Lord within the bread, and this verse was interpreted as the fact that a man has a body and soul and each of them is nourished by the bread, the body by the actual food in it and the soul by the Godly utterance in the bread, and this interpretation can be especially felt in Israel.

He is credited with the creation of the *Seder of Tu B'Shevat* (a festive meal in honor of the "Trees' New Year"), which was arranged to show the Jewish exiles the specific qualities, attributes, and holiness of the Israeli fruit. This Tu B'Shevat seder night illustrated the goodness of the Land of Israel and attracted Jews to go there. He wrote *Hemdat Hayamim*, a book in which he called the holiday Tu B'Shevat "the Day of Eating Fruit" and said the joy on Tu B'Shevat over everything that was given to us by God, according to the Torah, is full of secrets and so is the eating of fruits of four kinds.

Rabbi Bezalel Ashkenazi, his teacher, who was Egypt's chief rabbi, arrived in Israel in 1588 and served as a chief rabbi and leader of the Jerusalem community.

The *Aliyah* of the Pupils of Ha-Gaon (The Genius) Rabbi Eliyahu of Vilna (Hagra)

These followers of Hagra were the *mitnagdim* (opponents) of the Hasidim. They arrived from Lithuania thirty-one years after the Hasidic *aliyah*. Ten years earlier their leader, Hagra, who had yearned for many years to make *aliyah*, arrived at the Austrian border and decided to go back. The reason is unknown, although he is supposed to have said that he was not allowed to make *aliyah* to Israel. His pupils, however, arrived in Tiberias in 1808 with Rabbi Menachem of Shklov.

RABBI SHNEOUR ZALMAN OF LYADY:
"THE ENTIRE ISRAEL IS AN ATONEMENT ALTAR"

Rabbi Shneour, who is known as Ha'admor Hazaken and Baal HaTanya, the Old Admor (Admor is the abbreviation of the Hebrew *Adonenu Morenu ve Rabbenu*, meaning "master, teacher, and rabbi") and the author of the *Tanya*, was the first Admor of the Habad movement of Hasidism (*Habad Hasidut*). He was born in 1745 in Liozna, which was then Poland. He was a bright young student, and when he began to study the Kabbalah he became known as a Talmud prodigy. After his marriage, he arrived in Mezritch and studied the Torah with the Maggid (preacher) there. Eventually the Maggid's pupils began to lead the Hasidim, each in his own neighborhood. In Lithuania and Belarus, it was Rabbi Menachem Mendel of Vitebsk who was joined by Shneour of Lyady.

In 1776 the Rabbi of Vitebsk decided to make *aliyah* to Israel together with three hundred of his Hasidic followers. Shneour of Lyady was not decisive about the move because he feared leaving his congregation behind, and he cited the words of the Maggid of Mezritch about the Baal Shem Tov, Rabbi Israel ben Eliezer, the founder of Hasidic Judaism, who could not come to Israel: "There are souls that just need Israel and souls that need to live abroad."

However, after the group had left, Shneour decided to

join them. He took his pupils with him, and they traveled to Mogilev, where Rabbi Menachem Mendel and his followers were stopping over. It was Rabbi Menachem Mendel himself and his pupils who persuaded Shneour of Lyady to remain in Belarus and lead the Hasidic community there. He spent a week debating with himself, and finally he accepted the "verdict" to remain behind.

Despite his decision, he was very much attached to the Holy Land, and in one of his epistles to his Hasidim he wrote, "Israel is the greatest charity of all charities because Israel is the Altar of Atonement."

THE GREAT HASIDIC LEADERS

The Great Hasidic Leaders, lovers of Israel, added additional aspects to the obligation to make *aliyah* to Israel. Rabbi Yaakov Friedman, the Admor (Hasidic rabbi) of Husiatin, a border town between what was then Russia and Austria, was born in 1878 in Bohush, Romania, and was, on his father's side, a direct offspring of the Maggid of Mezritch and grandchild of Rabbi Israel of Rojin. His grandfather used to say: "When I ascend to Israel I shall be asked: Why have you come without your Jews? To which my answer will be: Because those whose generation has not been prepared for *aliyah* will remain in exile." This saying became his legacy for his sons and grandsons to prepare Jews to make *aliyah* to Israel and settle there.

Both Rabbi Friedman and Rabbi Yitzchak of Bohush were very active in encouraging Jews to settle in Israel. Rabbi Friedman was active in the *Hamizrachi* movement, participated in its meetings, and published letters and essays in praise of Zionism. He regarded the *Hamizrachi,* a movement devoted to bringing Jews to Israel and preparing the land for their settlement there, as being devoted to the Torah of Israel and to Israel, and he was faithful to that idea all his life. In 1937 he went to Israel, settling in Tel Aviv on Bialik Street, and set up his synagogue and study center there. In one of his early essays, in 1918, on the *halakhic* foundation for the issue of settling Israel, he said that the Ramban wrote in his book *Sefer Hamitzvoth,* "The Book of Mitzvoth," that the main mitzvah of settling Israel is of an agricultural character— plow, sow, and build. And someone else wrote that settling Israel is not a one-time mitzvah, it is an eternal one; and yet another wrote that he who dwells in Israel and recites the *Shema*, attends the *shachrith* and *arvit* (morning and evening) prayers, and speaks in *Lashon Hakodesh,* the Holy Language, *Ivrith* (Hebrew), gains *Olam Haba* (the World to Come).

The Ramban wrote in his explanation for a verse of the Song of Solomon that the People of Israel will go to Israel with the permission of the Nation's Kings, and in the Book of *Haredim* he wrote: "Every Jew should be fond of Israel and come to it from the ends of the world with great passion, as a son who returns to his mother's lap, and the Land of Israel will be salvaged through its redemption."

In another essay, published by Rabbi Yaakov Friedman in 1918 in the weekly *Hamizrachi* in Warsaw, he says:

> *We are a nation and not only a religious society, and this was already established in the biblical verse, And the LORD said unto her, Two nations are in thy womb, and two manner of people shall be separated from thy bowels (Genesis 25:23). Our religion is a national religion and the first commandment is linked with the deliverance of the Nation from Egypt: I am the LORD thy God, which have brought thee out of the land of*

Egypt, out of the house of bondage (Exodus 20:2). Nationality without a religion is insufficient for us and so is our religion; without a nationality it is not durable. We see free-thinking Jews (nonreligious, secular) who, when the national sentiment has been aroused in them, gradually come closer to the Torah and the commandments out of a liking, out of a wish to take part in and connect with. So why shouldn't we hope that they will attain it, perhaps only by chance rather than by purpose? And if someone will claim that Zionism is secular, then let us give it a Jewish (religious) character.

Rabbi Friedman's attitude toward secular Zionism was a loving and supportive one on the one hand, as well as firm on the other, seeing the lights but not ignoring the shades. He would bless the miracle of the foundation of the new state but also regretted its negative aspects. One of the issues that caused him the greatest sorrow was the question of "Who is a Jew?" which came up concerning the possibility of having civil marriage in the country. The idea of abolishing the holiness of marriage meant for him tearing out the roots of existence of the nation.

He ascribed such thoughts to a silliness that seized the people, and he said that a man will not commit an offense unless he is seized by silliness. If one lacks an opinion, will he be able to distinguish between opinions? In this state of mind one stops to distinguish between holiness and secularity, between the People of Israel and the other nations, between weekdays and the Sabbath. When he was asked how to fight those who base the spiritual construction in Israel on foreign foundations, he replied: "Not with weapons of hatred or slander."

A pupil of Rabbi Menachem Mendel of Lubavich tried

to maintain the saying, "Treat everyone humbly." However, once he saw a Jew in the market acting in a very base way, and he was embarrassed. How could he maintain his humility? He asked Rabbi Mendel and was answered: "You are besmirching this man's name and this is the worst you can do." "So, with what weapon should we fight them?" he asked. "With the same weapons that we are fighting our own passions—by qualifying in sanctity. If these people [the leaders of the Israeli settlement] do not accept our ways and opinions, this means that not everything is in order with us too. Let us bring our thoughts, speech, and deeds to a degree of holiness and then victory will come."

Rabbi Friedman, the Admor of the Husiatin Hasidic Jews, was a famously modest Torah scholar compared with the Ruzhin Hasidut, another Hasidic dynasty which was known for its splendor.

RABBI NAFTALI ZVI YEHUDA BERLIN, THE NATZIV

Another great figure of the Torah who loudly supported the *aliyah* to Israel was Rabbi Naftali Zvi Yehuda Berlin, otherwise known as Ha-Natziv or the Natziv from Volozhin, head of the Volozhin Yeshiva. Born in the town of Mir in Belarus in 1817, he came to Israel in 1853 and became one of the local Ashkenazi leaders of the *Yishuv*, the Jewish settlement in Israel before its independence. In Volozhin, he was married at a very young age, just after his bar mitzvah, to the daughter of Rabbi Yitzhak, the head of the Volozhin Yeshiva, and granddaughter of Rabbi Chaim of Volozhin. Rabbi Chaim was very much attached to Israel and headed the fund-raising for the *Perushim Kolel*, an institute for advanced study in Safed and Jerusalem, established there by pupils of Hagra (Ha-Gaon Rabbi Eliyahu from Vilna) after their *aliyah* to Israel, and most likely had great influence over the Natziv in this matter. These donations were given on the basis of the donors' wish to be part of the Holy Land and its land-dependent commandments.

The Natziv was a great supporter of the settlement enterprise in Israel and was an active member in the *Chibat Zion* (the Love of Zion) movement. He compared the present-day settlement, led by secular young people, to the Shivat Zion, the Return to Zion of the exiles from Babylonia in the time of Ezra, when some of the newcomers were married to foreign women and consecrated the Sabbath. He wrote that he "accepted" them because they prepared the towns for the settlement of the rest of the newcomers, until the land could fill up with its sons.

He wrote (in *Shivat Zion* 5, p. 17):

> *We must not think that it should have been done in a different way because we must not criticize God's deeds, as was explained by Isaiah: "My thoughts are not your thoughts and my ways are not your ways." Ezra the Scribe gathered a few thousand people in Babylonia of all kinds—from those great in the Torah to those who married Gentile women and were used to desecrating the Sabbath, to those who did not know the Torah at all. All these were gathered and prepared the settlement in Israel and eventually the country filled up with their sons. So must we, all kinds of Children of Israel, wake up to God's will.*

In 1886 the Natziv registered as a member of the Khibat Zion association and wrote in the movement's record book that the voice of God knocks on our hearts to say let me in, which was intended to mean: Donate money to the settlers of

Israel to help them build the country, because the hour has come to stop saying that Israel is deserted and abandoned.

His devotion to Israel was total; he would not hear bad things about it. Once he heard a *meshullakh* (a fund-collecting emissary for the upkeep of Torah study institutions) who returned from Israel reporting about what he saw there. The Natziv interrupted his report by shouting at him. "Get out of here, spy." The messenger assured him that everything he told him was true. However, the Natziv claimed that biblical spies didn't tell lies about Israel either. Nevertheless, it is still forbidden to speak badly of the Holy Land, even if it is true, and he who speaks badly about the land is considered a spy.

In 1890 he demanded action to settle Israel because it is God's will, saying that God changed the emperor's heart to permit the money collected to support our brethren in Israel.

MEIR SIMCHA HACOHEN OF DVINSK

Rabbi Meir Simcha of Dvinsk in Latvia is the author of the book *Happy Light* (*Or Sa'me'ach*), which is considered one of the best explanations of Maimonides' doctrine. He was asked by a special emissary from the Zionist *Histadrut* labor federation in Israel to write an address to the Jewish public urging the people to donate to *Keren Hayesod* (United Israel Appeal), which acted as an instrument to help to build the country. He wrote that Abraham our Father, after recognizing his creator, walked the length and width of Israel and planted a tamarisk tree (an *Eshel*); his son Isaac sowed the land and dug wells; and Isaac's son Jacob built a house there—all in the hope that their sons would dwell in this land, the land of Moriah. Since that day, he said, and since the day that our Holy Torah was given, the prophets never stopped ordering the settlement of the land. In the Torah there is no single portion that doesn't mention Israel; the mitzvah of settling Israel is equivalent to commandments that appear in the Torah.

Before he died, in Riga in 1926, friends came to see him. When they talked of Israel and the pioneers who went there to build, work, protect, and revive it, Rabbi Meir Simcha said: "When a Jew goes to Israel, he is already a good Jew."

Rabbi Eliezer Yehuda Waldenberg

Rabbi Eliezer Yehuda Waldenberg said, "Every Jew must make *aliyah* to Israel and settle in it." Even the greatest rabbinical judges of the generation spoke clearly about the importance of the mitzvah of making *aliyah* to Israel.

Rabbi Eliezer Yehuda Waldenberg was born in Jerusalem in 1915 and was appointed as a rabbinical judge *(dayan)*, and a judge of the *Bet Din Gadol* (Great Court) in 1981. His expertise was in resolving especially difficult divorce cases. His attitude was unique and matter of fact and ignored the accepted, and he approached the settlement of Israel in the same way. He explained the importance of this mitzvah by noting that it has two facets: a general one, which is the duty of all the people of Israel; and a personal one, which obliges each individual Jew. The general facet of the mitzvah stopped with the destruction of the Holy Temple. However, since God in his goodness has enabled us to settle in part of our land and the gates have been opened to us, this mitzvah has regained its general characteristic. Thus every Jewish community abroad must come together and settle in the land.

He goes on to explain that there is no reason to refuse to settle in Israel because it is led by secular Jews, or use the other excuse that salvation will not materialize through these non-God-fearing people. He comments that it would indeed be better if there were more God-fearing Jews in Israel but adds that we do not know the secret ways of the world; after all it is a fact that evil kings saved the People of Israel. For example, in the days of Yerovam II (Jeroboam II)—the king who sinned and made others sin—God expanded the borders of the Land of Israel and led it to prosperity, as in the time of King Solomon. After the horrible Holocaust, he said, we need all the capable people to build this country, no matter whether they are God-fearing or not.

He further quoted the words of the Hatam Sofer, one of the leading Orthodox rabbis in Europe in the early nineteenth century, about the commandment to work the land which is, in itself, a mitzvah because the Torah commands you to "gather your grain" and doing this cannot be delayed because of the Torah study. Rabbi Waldenberg also said that the Hatam Sofer's words are like gold, since this great Zionist was also an Orthodox Jew who normally would not dare express such things; the fact that he did only provides us with strength and reinforces our cause.

The Holocaust and the war left many of the great scholars with the single option, *aliyah* to Israel.

Rabbi Yitzchak Nisenbaum (1868–1942), who lived in Lithuania and died in the Warsaw Ghetto, joined the Chovevey Zion, a Zionist movement in Minsk in 1887, and later the "Nezach Israel" society, which aimed for the settlement of Israel on the basis of ethical and spiritual renovation. He was dedicated to the success of the first Zionist Congress and served as a mediator between Herzl and the Chovevey Zion movement in Russia. He encouraged the Jews to mobilize all their strength to fight all the torments with the only weapon they owned—the prayer for the coming salvation upon our land.

In the ghetto he was asked by Jews whether the Jews who died in the ghetto are considered by the *halakhah* as martyrs who died on *Kiddush Hashem* (sanctification of the name of God). His answer was remarkable. "This is the hour of the sanctification of God in life, not in death. In the past, our enemies demanded the soul, and the Jew sacrificed his body for the sanctification of the name of God. Now the deadly oppressor demands our body; therefore we must defend it, defend our life."

Spiritual leaders such as Rabbi Khalfon Moshe Hacohen of Jerba, an island opposite the coast of Tunisia, were enthusiastic about Zionism even without any anti-Semitic provocation coming from their neighbors.

Rabbi Hacohen (1874–1949), who was an offspring of a well-known family of rabbis, served as the rabbi of his native island, Jerba in Tunisia. After the establishment of the State of Israel, he arranged for a three-day celebration of the Independence of Israel. In his writings, prior to the establishment of the state, he included detailed political ideas not only for the Zionist cause, but also for cosmopolitan purposes, such as a suggestion to set up a United Nations organization and an International Court that would sit in Jerusalem. He advocated the Zionist idea of settling in Israel, citing the beautiful gift that God promised our ancestors. It is the cornerstone of the eternity of the Israeli nation and the observance of the Torah, he said, and everyone who assists in this helps it as well; as we see the built-up national home for the Jews, the glimpses of salvation begin to appear.

Rabbi Hacohen, while still in Jerba, bought a plot of land in Israel and intended to make *aliyah*, but his ill health compelled him to remain in Jerba, where he eventually died. However, after a complicated process, his body was brought to Jerusalem for burial in 2005.

The journalist and writer Shlomo Nakdimon, who was close to Rabbi Shlomo Goren, the chief rabbi of Israel as well as Zahal's chief rabbi for many years, heard from him that in his visits with the Lubavicher Rebbe in New York, Rabbi Goren questioned the rebbe several times about why he didn't make *aliyah* to Israel. To his usual answers—that if he went, he would not be able to leave it again, and that he has many roles and missions in the Jewish world—he added another: The Chabad rebbes need the graves of their ancestors to put in the requests they receive from their followers, since these graves are a source of holiness. While they lived in Russia, they did not go to the Land of Israel for this reason; however in the United States the first rebbe, who was the father-in-law of the late Menachem Mendel the Lubavicher, did go to Israel and visited the ancestors' graves in Hebron, and he absorbed holiness from them. But the next rebbe, the last Lubavicher—Menachem Mendel Schneersohn—already had a grave of his predecessor, so he did not need to go to Israel. Nakdimon said Rabbi Goren accepted and appreciated this answer.

Preferring exile over Israel has had repercussions—apart from guilt—that extend even to this day. Scholars, including those in our generation, have tried to find an excuse (a *teretz*, in Yiddish) to stay in the Diaspora. One of them was the late Rabbi Aharon Kotler, who was miraculously saved during the Second World War when he fled from Vilna, Lithuania, to Shanghai in China. Being one of the great scholars of present-day Charedim, an ultra-Orthodox sect, he could not decide, toward the end of the war, whether to go on to the United States, where he had been called to set up a big yeshiva, or to go to the Holy Land (this is pre-1948). His internal indecision between the mitzvah of settling in the Holy Land and going to a place where he was needed led him to take an unexpected action. He decided to leave his fate to a *Goral-Hagra* trial. Hagra (who was the Gaon Rabbi Eliyahu from Vilna) ruled that in difficult questions for which there is no clear answer, one should perform the following Kabbalah ceremony: Open the Bible to a random page and count the verses that eventually lead, so it seems, to a verse that provides the solution.

This ceremony, which is foreign to Judaism and not widely accepted, is rarely performed. Even so, a famous example from the twentieth century had been the case of Reb Aryeh Levin, who used it when it was impossible to identify twelve soldiers of the Convoy of 35, also known as *Lamed He* (*lamed he* means 35 in Hebrew), during the War of Independence. The convoy had gone to help fighters in the area of Gush Etzion and were all killed by the Arabs. Some of their bodies were so badly mutilated that they could not be identified. Reb Levin used this "trick," and he arrived at a verse that helped him to identify the twelve, according to names mentioned in the verse. The soldiers were then given a Jewish burial.

Rabbi Aharon Kotler cynically used the same ceremony to decide whether to go to America or to the Land of Israel.

The verse he found was "And God told Aharon: go to Moses, to the desert." America at the time was considered to be a Jewish spiritual desert, and Kotler eventually went to Lakewood, New Jersey, where he established a yeshiva. It seems absurd to mobilize fate in order to remain in the Diaspora.

· 14 ·

ALIYAH, ZIONISM, AND SALVATION

*U*NDOUBTEDLY, THE PERCEPTION of the Jerusalem Talmud and of the Israeli scholars during early times was that both saw in Israel the only option to maintain Jewish life despite its poor standing. In contrast, the Babylonian scholars granted themselves legitimacy to live in the Diaspora for reasons of convenience, authority, and power.

Even in the days of the Judges, when Israel was at a low point, the leaders of Israel considered leaving but didn't because their commitment was to the Holy Land. The Judges of Israel used this example to conclude that salvation is possible even when the nation is in an extremely low state: "This is what Otniel said: whether innocent or guilty, he must save them" (Rashi commentary on Judges 3:10).

Gideon said: "If they were evil, as he performed his wonders to them for nothing, he will do the same for us" (Rashi commentary on Judges 6:13). Ha-Malbim (acronym for Rabbi Meir Loeb ben Jehiel Michael Weisser) explains that this is why Gideon, upon going out to war, asked for a special sign from God. He also thought, at first, that salvation was impossible when the people had no rights.

And if we skip to Rabbi Yehuda Halevi (Rihal) in his philosophical book *Hakuzari* ("The Hazar"), he condemned those who were idle, and he delayed complete salvation. When the king of the Hazars asks why the Jewish People don't immigrate to Israel today, "the friend" [interlocutor] answers—criticizing those who consider only "their residence and business" and who think their prayers are something separate, a hypocrisy that resembles the parrot's chatter and the starling's twitter—"Indeed you have found my place of shame, the King of Hazar."

This is indeed the sin because of the designation that God assigned to the Second Temple. The Godly interest is supposed to apply to those today as it would have in Babylonian days, if all responded to the call to return willingly to Israel. But only a few agreed then, and the important people remained in Babylonia, accepting exile and servitude so long as they didn't have to relinquish their homes and businesses. You can find parallels to this day.

One heard a somewhat different opinion from Rabbi Eliezer Desler, the Lithuanian Orthodox rabbi, who stipulated that the *aliyah* to Israel required appropriate religious life there. He maintained that the *aliyah* is indeed the observance of the mitzvah to settle the Land of Israel but on condition that the Torah be totally observed. He added, though, that according to the signs given to us by Hazal (the Sages of Blessed Memory), our generation is the generation of the Messiah tracks, which means that we are about to observe the coming of the Messiah. He noted that we see that many Jews gather in Israel, relieved of their subjection to Gentiles, and the land yields its fruit.

Another contemporary Sephardic rabbi and a lover of the Zionist idea of settling the land is Rabbi Eliyahu Pardes (1893–1972), who was the chief rabbi of Jerusalem. His ancestors were expelled from Spain in 1492, came to Israel, and lived there ever since, and they were great Torah scholars.

Rabbi Pardes, who was a member of the *Chalutzey Hamizrach* (Pioneers of the East), and in contrast to other Sephardic Jews even served in the Turkish Army in the First World War, was later head of the Porat Yoseph Yeshiva and a teacher and schoolmaster of several schools. He compared the contemporary exile of his time to that of the exile in Egypt, an exile that affected the entity of Israel. He said that God gave Israel three good gifts and all of them were given through agonies: the Torah, Israel, and *Olam Haba* (the World to Come), and all three of them are holy. Israel and especially Jerusalem, its eternal capital, is holy because it is said: *for out of Zion shall go forth the law, and the word of the Lord from Jerusalem* (Isaiah 2:3). Israel, because of its holiness and supremacy, does not tolerate indecent deeds and expels those people who will imitate the Gentiles' abominations. Agonies are the crucible that purifies man's body and soul and lifts him closer to his creator, and thus he is privileged to inherit the land, and this is how and why we obtained the three gifts: the Torah, the Land of Israel, and the World to Come.

Why does the Salvation of Israel come through secular people rather than by means of the observant?

Rabbi Eliezer Waldenberg, mentioned earlier, supported the idea of *aliyah* and settlement even if it was administered by secular rule and nonobservant people, rather than no *aliyah* and no settlement at all. He also dismissed the claim that it is impossible for salvation to happen for people who have no fear of God in their hearts. *Aliyah* is a positive step. The more religious Jews arrive in Israel, the more influence they will have there, he argues, so any way of making *aliyah* is for the best. And in any case, who can question God's deeds? It is told in the Bible (Kings) that God sent us his help through a sinful King of Israel (Yerovam), who waged wars on his neighbors and expanded the country, a favorable outcome, once again proving that "an offense does not erase a mitzvah."

It should be pointed out that the return to Israel of the Babylonian Jews was granted by a Gentile king, Koresh, which showed that the salvation of Israel is so important that it could be achieved through non-Jews as well.

We have already noted that the Babylonian scholars made excuses for not making the return, pointing to the poor spiritual level in Israel as justification for their remaining in their comfortable nest. The Orthodox adopted this line of thought in recent centuries and ignored the idea that salvation arrives in stages.

When the late Rav Kook was asked how he could interact with secular Jews and conduct a dialogue with them, since they ate unclean food and slept with unclean women, he replied, "In the Kaddish prayer we say *yitgadal ve'itkadash*, that is, first we will grow and then we will sanctify."

A DOUBLE CONSOLATION

The Habad movement considered *aliyah* a very important mitzvah. The consolation for the destruction of the Temple and the Exile appears in a double expression: *Nachamu, Nachamu Ami* ("Be consoled, be consoled, my People.") (Isaiah 40:1). The Midrash (*Yalkut Shimoni Isaiah*, op.cit.; *Eicha Raba*, end of *Parasha a*) explains it this way: "They were twice stricken and they are twice consoled." What is the meaning of this double consolation: in what way will it be double?

There is double consolation in a *quantitative* meaning. For example, a person whose home was burned down in a fire will be consoled by another home he builds in its place. And if the new home is twice as big as the old one and more luxurious as well, this will be a double consolation, double in quantity. However, there is a consolation double in *quality* as well. A regular consolation provides compensation but maintains the sorrow and the grief. But a double consolation erases the sorrow altogether and reveals that what seemed like a painful and grieving event was in fact good (*Likutey Sichot*, vol. 29, p. 377).

An example is seen in the Gemara story (*Ta'anit* 21a; *Sanhedrin* 108b) about Nachum Ish Gamzu, who was carrying a gift to the Caesar. Along the way, an innkeeper replaced the contents of the box with sand. When the Caesar opened his gift, he was furious and wanted to kill Nachum, seemingly a negative and sorrowful situation. However, Nachum believed that even this was for the best (in Hebrew: *Gam zu le'tova*). And indeed, eventually a miracle occurred and the sand was turned into a weapon by which the Caesar defeated his enemies. Nachum was rewarded generously. So in the end it transpired that the exchange of the box contents with sand was not a negative but the opposite, a marvelous positive that was not recognized as such at the beginning. This is therefore a double consolation—a consolation that reveals that there was nothing bad about what took place but rather the opposite—pure goodness.

Another illustration can be found in the Gemara story (last page of *Makot*) about Rabbi Akiva and his friends, who came to Jerusalem and saw a fox coming out of the Holy of Holies, the Temple. Rabbi Akiva's friends wept at the sight, but Akiva laughed.

"Why are you laughing?" they asked.

"Why are you weeping?" he replied.

They answered that it was written "and the stranger who comes near will be killed" and now foxes walk about there. Isn't that a reason to weep?

Akiva explained that he sees in the fox a realization of Uria's prophecy—"Zion will be ploughed to a field." Therefore he is now certain that Zecharia's prophecy—"Old men and women will be sitting in the streets of Jerusalem"—will materialize.

The friends told him: Akiva, you have consoled us, Akiva you have consoled us.

This story expresses the double consolation which is linked with a double stroke: not only the destruction of the Temple but also the blasphemy of a fox roving in the Holy of Holies. However, Akiva is displaying joy because he is able to see in his mind the double consolation that stems from the height of the destruction, a consolation that will completely erase the sorrow and pain, and furthermore turn into a source of joy and happiness.

This kind of consolation could not be understood in the time of the exile. The reasoning goes that if we had been able to see the goodness in the exile, we would be sorrowful about it and beg God to deliver us from it. Therefore God created a reality in which the exile with its troubles seemed completely bad, so that our attitude toward it would be totally negative. However, when deliverance arrives, then the double consolation will arrive as well, a double consolation which is now beyond our perception; only then shall we see and feel the goodness that was concealed in the exile.

In the future our eyes shall open and we will understand that even the darkest events of the exile, even the excessive humiliation of the honor of God and Israel, were nothing but a concealed goodness that will reveal itself at the time of the redemption. Then we shall understand that even the horrors of exile have derived from the "concealed graces" of God and we shall thank him for that: *Odcha Adonai ki Anafta bi* ("I shall thank you, God, for being angry with me") (Isaiah 12:1). This is the double consolation, a consolation that turns sorrow to goodness (*Likutey Sichot*, vol. 19, p. 67).

How Will the Salvation (*Geula*) Appear?

Rabbi Hiyya Rova and Rabbi Shimon ben Halafta were walking in the Arbel valley and saw the dawn rising. Rabbi Hiyya said to Rabbi Shimon: "So does the salvation of Israel start bit by bit and gradually illuminate more and more." And what is the reason for that? And he explained using the following example from *Megillat* Esther: at first

"Mordechai would sit at the King's gate," then "facing the King's gate," after which "Haman took the clothes and the horse," etc. After that: "and Mordechai left the king dressed in courtly dress." And finally: "and the Jews had light and merriment."

And also, "when Israel ate the Pesach (Passover) meal, they ate it in a hurry," but further on in the future they were told: "You will not leave in a hurry, and you will not escape" (*Shemot* [Exodus] *Rabbah* 19).

> *12: Therefore prophesy and say unto them, Thus saith the Lord GOD; Behold, O my people, I will open your graves, and cause you to come up out of your graves, and bring you into the Land of Israel.*

> *13: And ye shall know that I am the LORD, when I have opened your graves, O my people, and brought you up out of your graves,*

> *14: And shall put my spirit in you, and ye shall live, and I shall place you in your own land: then shall ye know that I the LORD have spoken it, and performed it, saith the LORD. (Ezekial 37)*

The late Rabbi Eliezer Waldenberg takes us to the time and regions following the Holocaust:

> *Who will guarantee to us that we, after the enormous extermination done by Hitler Yimach Shmo ("may his name be erased"), the oppressor of humanity, when we were in a state of "nothing and abandonment and helpless," were not the same as in those days? It seems that never had there been such an extermination since the creation of man. Therefore we must know that in God's grace to us He did not mean to efface us off the land, and that is why we immediately, like air for breathing,*

need an independent state on firm ground in our land, and God
helped us in His great mercy through those who held the helm
of the national leadership and were ready and skilled to do so,
without looking at the fact that most of them were not obser-
vant. It is we who mainly must do our duty and keep all the
mitzvot and among them the greatest mitzvah of all, aliyah,
and settlement of the land which equates to all the mitzvot in
the Torah, and we must influence as much as we can everything
which is called Israel, within the state's institutions and outside
them, in the town and in the countryside. (Tzitz Eliezer)

Rabbi Teichtel in his book *Em Ha-Banim Smecha* ("The
Mother of the Sons Is Glad") conducts a genuine account-
ing of the Orthodox Jews and concludes that the return to
Israel is the real repentance. Teichtel postulates that even if
they suffer troubles, they must not leave God and the Holy
Land, and that their main sin was going to Egypt. And now,
in our times, after the most nonobservant Jews returned to
our land and gave their souls for it, and did not wish for
another country, this is definitely considered to be repentance (*teshuvah*) in the eyes of God. Why didn't these Jews
keep the Torah commandments? It is because they were
not brought up or educated to do so, and they resembled a
baby who had been captured by Gentiles. Because Orthodox Jews did not toil for the building of the country, they
had no influence upon it and the influence was by those
who toiled and built it; they are its rulers. Who knows if
the Orthodox Jews will ever be able to justify themselves
to the Heavenly Supreme Court as to why they did not take
part in the construction of the land movement?

According to Teichtel, if the Orthodox Jews (the *haredim*)
had taken part in its development, the Holy Land would

look completely different, and it would be a much holier place. However, after having distanced themselves from it, they must not wonder and ask questions why Israel is the way it is, because they have only themselves to blame.

No less firm about this matter was Dr. Isaac Breuer (the grandson of Rabbi Samson Raphael Hirsch, the innovator of Orthodoxy in Germany), a scholar, philosopher, and politician, one of the leaders of Orthodox Jewry before the establishment of the State of Israel, one of the founders of Agudat Israel party, and one of the presidents of Poalei Agudat Israel party. At first he objected strongly to secular Zionism, which in his eyes repudiated God's authority and Torah. However, after at first doubting the future of the national enterprise, he eventually demanded to put the settlement of Israel at the top of the Agudat Israel's agenda and make the country the life center of Jewry.

Nevertheless, despite the practical change of his attitude, he never stopped criticizing the secular nationalism of Zionism, but not the practical activity of the Zionists. He immigrated to Israel in 1936 and settled in Jerusalem, intending to devote himself to the issues of Agudat Israel and bring about his idea of founding a national home in Israel for Jewry. In the book *Yada'nu Derech* (a new editon edited by Shmuel Chen, Mossad Harav Kook, 2007), Rabbi Breuer is revealed as a man with independent thought and a fighter for his ideas.

Breuer was very aware of the historical processes affecting the people of Israel, namely the strengthening of the Zionist movement and the Balfour Declaration, which recognized the rights of the Jewish people to settle in the Holy Land, and he was worried lest the indifference of Orthodox Jewry harm the spiritual character of the future Jewish state. In fact he very strongly criticized the leadership of Agudat Israel for its indifference: Does not Orthodox Jewry feel the huge responsibility lying on its shoulders? Doesn't it realize that the Jewish National Home could possibly turn out to be the most horrible national trouble, or it could be the hopeful beginning of a happier future? Does it not comprehend that the struggle for Torah's national rule, which would press its characteristic impression on the entire Jewish period of our time, did not take place more clearly and fervently anywhere other than in the Jewish National Home?

Breuer was a sharp and realistic polemicist. His second visit to Israel in winter of 1933-1934 impressed him deeply. The extended construction and the flourishing agriculture led him to the conclusion that "the curse that has laid on this land has been removed in our time, and that Israel has begun to shake off its magic slumber, and new life is bursting out everywhere in it."

He of all people, the Orthodox leader, compared the indifference of the Babylonian leaders to what was happening in life in Israel to the cold attitude shown by his Orthodox colleagues and partners toward the leadership of the *Yishuv Yashan* (Jewish life in the Holy Land before the modern Zionist movement), to the developing processes that were taking place in Israel. In a most vehement speech he gave in Frankfurt following his visit to the Holy Land, he criticized even more sharply the disregard of the Orthodox leadership for the historical processes affecting the people of Israel and their withdrawal of the Yishuv Yashan from the developing life in Israel. Breuer explained in his speech that in contrast to the old perceptions of a miraculous salvation, the development of things in our days does not conform to our forefathers' imagination. Life has erupted in the land and we see with our very own eyes that it occurs in a way that is different, and even before the arrival of salvation, the country is adopting the practical way of life slowly but surely, and the veteran settlers are not taking part in it.

He appealed to the leaders of Agudat Israel, who included all international Orthodox Jewry, to let people know openly their attitude toward contemporary historical events. To him the right way was very clear: The route ascending to Jerusalem is only through Torah. The new generation will sooner or later find its destination in Israel. If the Jewish people faithful to the Torah establish in due time their clear relationship with Israel, the state of our youngsters will not be so hard as it is today. We must be responsible for the younger generation. The entire educational trend must change, it must become: Torah with Derech Israel. (This is a brilliant pun on Torah and Derech Eretz, which is Torah and politeness. *Derech* means a way, a route, and in this case it's a way of life, manners, customs, and conduct.)

A SOCIALIST AND A UNIVERSALIST

Although Breuer was a visionary politician and very much wanted to see the Torah state established in Israel, he understood clearly that the reality would be different. In his essay "On the Jewish State and the Torah Front," he strongly criticized the members of Agudat Israel for their lack of involvement in determining the Jewish character of the town of Tel Aviv. He also claimed that the Aguda's segregation of Orthodox from non-Orthodox and the differentiation between a Jewish community and politics, economics, and a compre-

hensive activity are but an exilic phenomenon. He understood that the Aguda adopted the segregationist model of the
Orthodox community that was created by his grandfather,
Rabbi Samson Raphael Hirsch, as a mechanism for distancing themselves from the Reform community, but he stressed
that "nonparticipation" is irrelevant for an existing Jewish
town and for a forthcoming Jewish State. "Clinging to the
segregation principle is but a petrification of the Aguda and
an external orthodoxy."

Breuer was well aware of the fact that the future Jewish
state would be a secular one. "One cannot assume that a
majority will be found in the country that would compel
the eternal authority of the Torah on the three authorities
of the state. If a state were to be established in our time, we
shall have to fight for its Jewish character." He therefore
demanded for the Torah-keepers' public, "a reduction in the
supreme will in the state, up to a measure of ability to live a
public life according to the Torah and the ability to develop
Torah culture within this public life."

By the way, this disregard, lack of involvement, and segregation and the establishment of the inner ghetto of the Yishuv
Yashan eventually gave birth to the first political assassina-
tion in the history of the new settlement in Israel, in 1924.
Dr. Israel de-Haan, a Dutch Jew who was the spokesman of
Orthodox Jewry and the right hand of Rabbi Sonnenfeld,
the Orthodox leader, was murdered by the Haganna people
upon the order of Yitzchak ben Zvi (who would become the
second president of Israel) and his wife Rachel Yanait. The
Haganna leaders could not bear the fact that the Orthodox
had turned their back on the new settlement efforts to set
up a Jewish establishment and to try to found a Jewish state

in the Holy Land. The climax was when Rabbi Sonnenfeld and de-Haan went off to the Arab desert to meet with King Faisal, where they declared that they preferred to live under his rule rather than under the secular Jewish leadership. After the verdict declared against him—researchers of the period think that Ben Gurion agreed to *Parashat De-Haan* ("The De-Haan Affair," by Shlomo Nakdimon and Saul Mayzlish, Modan, 1990)—three Haganna people, headed by Abraham Tehomi, ambushed him in the dark. When he came out from praying in the Heichal Shaarei Zedek synagogue on Jaffa Street in Jerusalem, they shot him three times, killing him. Orthodox circles of the period established a group called "The Holy De-Haan."

Tzaddikim (the righteous) who conform to the requirements of the law but nevertheless who are nonbelievers are the reason for skepticism, maintains Rabbi Yehuda Zvi Kook, the son of the Rav Kook and head of the Merkaz Ha-Rav Yeshiva in Jerusalem. How come so many great men in the Torah have so little preparation for faith? It is a fact that many of them neglected to study their faith. And another question: Why is it that such a grand generation is so complicated? His answer: The bigger it is, the more complicated it is. It is easier to travel in a cart with horses than to fly in an airplane. This is a terrible generation in all its issues and mix-ups, but also grand and extremely idealistic and full of devotion, says Kook.

In the Ten Commandments, which are the nucleus of our existence, the only commandment containing the reward for its performance is the Fifth Commandment: "Honor thy father and thy mother: that thy days may be long upon the land which the Lord, thy God, giveth thee." In other words, follow this commandment and you will prolong your lives in the Land of Israel.

Why does this commandment contain a reward? And why does the Torah emphasize "the land which the Lord thy God giveth thee"? Because this is Israel. And why does the Torah emphasize the element of Israel? First, to emphasize its importance, and second, to stress that all the other mitzvahs are not territorial and are beyond time and place.

This particular commandment links the first body of commandments, which are between Man and God, and the second body, which are between Man and his fellow-men. The reward in the Fifth Commandment is intended to stress, to the younger generation who arrived in Israel after the forty years of their parents' generation's wanderings in the desert, that their parents prepared the ground for their arrival and settlement in Israel, and they should be respected and not scorned for their forty years of unproductive travels. The importance of Israel in this case is the dominant commandment in the life of a Jew.

It is necessary to ask why the rabbis of the Diaspora who were brilliant scholars never adhered to the language of this commandment. One can assume that they understood its meaning very clearly and felt guilt for not observing it. Instead they preferred to rationalize their life in the Diaspora.

Rabbi Yochanan said: "*Kibbutz Galuyot* [the gathering of all the exiles in Israel] is as great as the creation day of the skies and the land," and indeed his saying goes deep into our chief problem—the interaction between the Land of Israel and the Diaspora; this interaction will decide the fate of the nation. This was true also in the days of the original *Shivat Zion*.

In contrast to ancient Greece and the Roman Empire, which have disappeared from the stage of history, Israel is *Chai ve-Kayam*, "alive and kicking," having restored its political and cultural life in its historical language on its historical land.

However, in the present generation there are other opinions as well. While the dominant one still reflects that of Rabbi Yochanan's above, there are others who think, from a realistic Zionism angle, that the Diaspora will be able to immunize itself against assimilation and degeneration via the strength of the new State of Israel which will project its political and cultural independence upon it.

Epilogue

IN THE VOYAGE we just completed, we hoped to provide insights into the age of the Talmuds and their contributions to the Jewish enterprise which have endured for two thousand years to the present. Inside and outside the Holy Land, the intellectualizations of the Talmudists were remarkable and dazzling. And, as we have shown, there was a tremendous battle for hegemony between the Jerusalem and Babylonian Talmudists, a battle won, for the most part, by the Babylonians. But was there a cost to the fundamental principles of the Jewish faith, which connected the land to the religion? And if it was transformative of basic Judaic principles (faith and land), was there guilt on the part of the

Babylonian Talmudists in order for them to preserve the essence of Judaism without the land?

We believe the earlier pages here confirm one of the basic principles of Torah Judaism: Land–Temple–People. As we have discovered in earlier chapters, an observant Jew is duty-bound to comply with 613 mitzvahs (*Taryag Mitzvoth*). One of these mitzvahs is the obligation to live physically in the Land of Israel, the Holy Land. In order to maintain their domicile outside the Holy Land, the Babylonian Talmudists tried to circumvent this commandment by brilliant rationalization and extension of the interpretation of the Torah. Yet their rationalizations contributed greatly to Torah Judaism and thus helped sustain the life of Judaism around the world.

According to basic psychological theory, "guilt" may be either individual or collective, and it stems from having made a grave error or committing an offense. Most of the time these feelings refer to people who feel a genuine and objective remorse for having breached a rule, even though they may have done so because of circumstances beyond their control. (Ironically, one could argue that guilt doesn't always have a negative impact on Jews, because there are many who think that guilt inspires overachievement. Perhaps the fact that guilt is part of the Jewish culture explains why so many Jews became exceptional personalities and leaders in such fields as science, business, art, and theater. It is readily known that almost a quarter, 23 percent, of Nobel Prize winners were of Jewish ancestry, yet Jews comprise only a quarter of one percent of the world population.)

The mitzvah of settling in the Land of Israel was in conflict with orders to abandon the land by a succession of conquering rulers. Even when rulers did not demand evacuation, they created such hardships that the Jews fled their harsh supervision to make a life elsewhere in a more peaceful environment. Nevertheless, they were aware that to live in the Land of Israel was one of the Torah's commandments. This is why the Babylonian Jewish community leaders used to exchange emissaries with Israel regarding *halakhah* and other critical interpretations of biblical text and provided support—both physical and spiritual—thus blunting the sting of their guilt over their abandonment of the Holy Land.

Throughout the centuries of the Diaspora, up to the present date, and particularly very strongly in the United States, one of the most powerful arguments that rabbis and other Jewish leaders used for *not* coming to the Holy Land was what we shall call the doctrine of the "Three Oaths." These oaths were collected from various sources in the Mishnah and the Gemara and enabled Jews to justify living outside of the Holy Land.

1. TO CLIMB THE GATED CITY: The prime argument used up to the present by many Hasidic factions is that until the Messiah comes and redemption takes place, it is unnecessary and perhaps forbidden to be a citizen of a country established in the Holy Land, because you are inhabiting a land which is not based on the fundamentals of the *halakhah*. The doctrine of "to climb the gated city" essentially means that it is impossible and unachievable. Therefore, these religionists (usually the ultra Orthodox) conclude, it is a reason for not living in Israel. Or if they do live in Israel, they do not consider the State of Israel as the Holy Land. Once again we see the elasticity of Jewish intellect and rationalization.

2. DUTY TOWARD JEWS IN THE DIASPORA: Further to this was the argument that since there were large populations of Jews living beyond Israel's borders, the rabbis and leaders were obliged to care for the spiritual, social, and intellectual needs of these people outside of the Holy Land.

3. A SYMBOL WILL SUFFICE: As we recounted here, there was a big dispute between Maimonides and Nachmanides. Maimonides, who was doing exceptionally well in Cairo, rationalized that one need not physically live in the Holy Land but could use a symbol or a gesture—as Jews do today by planting a tree in Israel—which would satisfy the mitzvah. Those who abided by the beliefs of the Ramban (Nachmanides), who came to dwell in Israel, totally disagreed and maintained that you must live in the Holy Land, for not only was it ordained in the Torah but the Holy Land has inimitable qualities which are holy, not only in the land but in the spiritual aspects of the air itself.

Most rabbis and leaders outside the Holy Land today adhere to Maimonides' belief that a symbol will suffice, which may help them to overcome what we refer to as "Jewish guilt." So the question arises: Do these followers of Maimonides who wish to be observant of all of the mitzvahs help to illuminate the history behind the phenomenon of Jewish guilt? The authors take no position, positively or negatively, with respect to this issue. We have no definitive answer to this very fundamental question. Our purpose in this book was to examine and, one hopes, shed light on the intriguing history of the time when the competing Jerusalem Talmud and Babylonian Talmud were developed, and to apprise readers of the complex arguments and brilliant rationalizations that took place between the rabbis in the Holy Land, the progenitors of the Jerusalem Talmud, versus those in the Diaspora who contributed to the Babylonian Talmud.

There is a famous Talmudic expression which was put forth by the rabbis after they could find no answer for a question or faced an issue that could not be resolved. The word used in the Talmud is *Teiku*, an abbreviation for *Tishbi Yetarez Kushiot u'Be'ayot*, which means that Elijah—the prophet Eliyahu Hatishbi—will resolve all unresolved problems. (The Hebrew word *teiku* also means a tie, as in a game or competition, and is used in football games.)

Teiku tells us in English that "only the prophet in the world to come will be capable of resolving the unresolvable." It is a fascinating concept which clearly expresses the beauty of Judaism as a religion because it accepts humility as one of its fundamental principles. We don't always know all the answers. Unfortunately, some rabbinical authorities tend to forget this very vital aspect of Judaism and become overly authoritative. We have to ask: Does this conduct violate the real meaning of humility in Judaism? And is not humility an integral part of spirituality?

Today there is a revival in the study of the Jerusalem Talmud, promoted, among others, by the late Rabbi Goren and Rabbi Adin Steinsaltz. Could this renaissance be attributed to Jewish guilt? Many scholars today believe that their predecessors may have slipped up by focusing on the Bet Midrash, the house of study, rather than the *Bet Ha-Kneset*, the synagogue, as the center of Jewish life, thus placing a higher priority on learning and prayer over prayer alone.

However, this idea, in effect, advanced the fundamental nature of Judaism. Consequently, the Babylonian Talmudists and other Diaspora communities which followed created a "new Judaism" which kept the faith and religion alive for two thousand years.

What the future will say, we don't know. However, based on precedent, we would hazard a clever and emotional prediction that Judaism will remain vibrant, alive for eternity, and continue to be subjected to superior intellectual arguments, which is one of the greatest assets, or perhaps *the* greatest, of the achievement called Judaism. To some it will incorporate culture and history and tradition. To others it will mean unbridled faith in the Torah and the absolute necessity of obedience to the mitzvahs. To still others, it will be a cerebral exercise without all of the affirmation. Regardless of which direction a Jew in the future will follow, the one thing that will likely endure in some form or other is the spirit—or perhaps we should say specter—of Jewish guilt. While the authors propose no scientific proof that this was a characteristic of the Babylonian Talmudists which became a genetic and subconscious element within the Jewish people, we hope this book will generate for the readers self-examination as to whether they possess a vestige of Jewish guilt, and the eagerness to explore its sources.

GLOSSARY

ARAMAIC—A northern Semitic language closely related to Hebrew which served as the official language of the Ancient Persian Empire. It is mentioned in the Bible as a language understood by the leaders of Judea in the time of the First Temple. During the Second Temple the Jews returning from Babylonia brought Aramaic to the Land of Israel and it became the trade and official language in the country, ousting the Hebrew language from the towns. The square Hebrew script which eventually replaced the ancient Hebrew script evolved from the Aramaic. The Babylonian Talmud is written in an Eastern dialect of Aramaic while the Jerusalem Talmud is written in a Western dialect. Aramaic penetrated the liturgy: The *Kaddish*, the *Kol Nidrei,* and the opening of the Passover Haggadah are in

Aramaic. Aramaic is still spoken in various communities.

ASHKENAZI COMMUNITIES—From the mid-ninth century—
Gaonic period—the name Ashkenaz became identified with
Germany. Jewish communal and social life as well as Jewish
scholarship developed in Christian Europe from the three
Rhineland communities of Spire, Worms, and Mainz in the
tenth century, then spread westward to France through Rashi
and his descendants and eastward to Germany and Bohemia,
establishing a unity of custom. Ashkenazi ritual and law differed from the parallel tradition developing in what was then
Moslem Europe—Spain. As a result, the word *Ashkenaz* became
applied to a religious and cultural tradition of those who followed the custom that originated among German Jews. With the
drift of German Jews over the eastern borders of their country
into the Slavic lands in the sixteenth century, and the adoption
by the Jews in those countries of the traditions and language
(Yiddish) of the German Jews, the word *Ashkenaz* received an
even wider connotation.

BAAL SHEM TOV (HA-BESHT), RABBI ISRAEL (1700–1760)—
Founder of the Hasidic movement. Born in the Ukraine to a
poor family and became an orphan at an early age. As a young
man he traveled through small towns, healing the sick with
herbs and amulets. After his marriage he retired to solitude and
meditation in the woods in Podolia. He felt he had a mission to
stir the hearts of those seeking communion with God. He did so
through praying while trembling. The emphasis on "intention"
(*kavanah*) was a further basic tenet of the Besht. True prayer was
pictured as a state which freed the personality from the tram-
mels of the body and allowed fusion of the soul with God. He
received his name because of good deeds to the poor. *Shem Tov*
literally means "good name" in Hebrew.

BAR KOKHBA—Leader of the rebellion against the Romans in 132–35 CE. Many, including Rabbi Akiva, thought he was the Messiah King (some sages denied this and called him Bar Koziva— liar). For a short while the Jews liberated Judea, and Bar Kokhba served as the president. However, the Romans mobilized large troops from far off and defeated Bar Kokhba's army. The Romans wanted to annul the national uniqueness of the Jews and therefore prohibited the study of the Torah, the gathering in synagogues, and the celebration of Sabbath and holidays. Almost everybody continued to observe the mitzvahs in secrecy, and the braver ones in the open, but those who were caught became martyrs.

BEN MAIMON, MOSES (MAIMONIDES OR RAMBAM) (1135–1204)— Philosopher and codifier, born in Spain but lived most of his life in Egypt, where he was physician to the court. Maimonides wrote several books. In *Mishne Torah* (Second Torah) or *Yad Hahazaka* (The Strong Hand), which he wrote in Hebrew, he summed up the laws and commandments of the Torah. The book became a standard work of Jewish law and a major source for subsequent codes. Even more significant in many respects was his book *Moreh Nevuchim* (Guide for the Perplexed), in which he wrote about the principal theological problems of Judaism, a book that was written for those who follow both Torah and philosophy and who are "perplexed" by the contradictions between the teachings of the two. Naturally this book provoked a storm of Orthodox protest accusing the Rambam of (at least) encouraging heresy, but finally the name of the Rambam became established as the symbol of the pure and orthodox faith; and the inscription on his tombstone says it all: "From Moses to Moses there was none like unto Moses."

BEN NACHMAN, MOSES (NACHMANIDES OR RAMBAN) (1194–1270)—Spanish Talmudist, Kabbalist, philosopher, and physician. Born in Girona, he was leader of Spanish Jewry and an early influence on Spanish Kabbalah, expressing his conservative beliefs on the need to adhere to the wisdom of earlier authorities. Following the Disputation of Barcelona—a debate with the apostate Paulus Christiani, a contest in which the Ramban was victorious, even earning a gift from the king—he was pursued by the Dominicans and charged with abuses against Christianity. He escaped from Spain to the Holy Land, where he became the spiritual leader of the Jewish community in Acre. He differed with Maimonides on the subject of the mitzvah of living in the Holy Land; Nachmanides believed the resettlement of the Land of Israel to be a biblical imperative, not one for which a symbol would suffice.

Bet Din [Heb. "house of judgment, court"]—Jewish court of law guided by the principles of the official *halakhah* in dealing with matters of civil, criminal, or religious law. The judges received their authorization from the heads of the yeshivas or from the Patriarch. A higher court, sometimes called "small Sanhedrin," consisted of twenty-three judges and was empowered to judge criminal cases. The highest type of court was known as the Great Bet Din or Sanhedrin.

Bet Midrash [Heb. "house of study"]—Place for study of the Law, and more specifically, of the rabbinic texts such as the Mishnah, Talmud, Codes, and Responsa. In the Talmudic Period the term *Bet Hamidrash* was almost synonymous with that of *yeshiva*. Its sanctity was considered greater than that of the synagogue, and rabbis of the Talmud preferred to pray there rather than adjourning to the synagogue. During medieval times it became close to the *Bet Knesset* (Synagogue) usually situated in the same building or close by. In Eastern Europe it was termed *kloize*. It was here that senior students would spend most of their day either in individual study or under the discipline of a Rosh Yeshiva or head of the academy.

CANAAN; LAND OF CANAAN—The ancient name of the area of southern Syria and Palestine. In the Bible, Canaan is the name of one of Ham's sons, grandson of Noah. According to the Bible, the land of Canaan was promised to Abraham and his descendants.

EVIL EYE ("A GRUDGING EYE")—A widespread and still extant superstition that the malignant and envious eye of an ill-disposed person can cause harm. Formulas were drawn up to be said in times of prosperity in order to ward off any evil eye (cf. the Yiddish phrase *kainehora,* "without an evil eye").

GAON—The denomination of the heads of the Babylonian yeshivas, at Sura and Pumbedita (600–1040).The *geonim* were actually the spiritual leaders of all the Diaspora at the time.

GEMARA [ARAMAIC "TRADITION" OR "STUDYING"]—The usual designation for the comment on and discussions around the Mishnah. The Mishnah together with the Gemara make up the Talmud. There is a Babylonian Gemara and a Jerusalem Gemara.

HAGGADAH ("NARRATION")—The set form in which the story of the Exodus must be told on the first two nights of Passover (in Israel, only on the first night) as part of the ritual "seder" (order) of these nights.

HALAKHAH [HEB. "LAW"]—That part of Jewish literature, stemming especially from the Talmudic and later periods, which deals with religious, ethical, civil, and criminal law. The plural, *halakhot,* is often used to refer to a collection of laws.

HAREDI [HEB. "REVERENTLY FEARFUL"]—Ultra-Orthodox Jews (plural: *haredim*), living mainly in Israel and the United States who speak Yiddish, are proponents of tradition, and consider themselves the only "authentic" Jews. They often reject secular culture, live in segregated neighborhoods, and dress in ways that set them apart from the general population. They are roughly divided into two subcultures, those who are Hasidic and those who are *benei yeshiva*, the followers of a particular Jewish academy and the scholar who heads it.

HASIDIC—Belonging to the Hasidut movement (Hasidism), a religious and social movement established by Rabbi Israel Baal Shem Tov around 1700 among the Jews in the Ukraine and Podolia; it later spread into other Eastern European countries. Nowadays it is found mainly in Israel and in the United States, and lately it has become worldwide. The main novelty of the Hasidut movement was its emphasis on the idea that everyone, whether a scholar or ignorant, can become a "Hasid"—a person of great piety and fervor and therefore a favorite of God, if only he will keep directing his thought to the love of God and accept the instructive authority of the Tzaddik (leader of the congregation).

ISRAELI KNESSET—The Israeli Parliament, seated in Jerusalem.

KABBALAH—In the thirteenth century the term came to be applied to the new mystical doctrines and systems that had been developing in southern France and Spain since the twelfth century and which reached their literary climax in the *Book of Zohar*.

MARRANOS—Fourteenth- and fifteenth-century Sephardic Jews of the Iberian peninsula who were forcibly converted to Christianity under threat of expulsion but who secretly continued to practice Judaism. During the Inquisition their descendants were relentlessly hunted down in Spain. The term is synonymous with "Converso" but carries a negative connotation since it was originally derived from the Spanish for "pig" and possibly from the Arabic *mahran* for "forbidden."

MASSEKHET—A tractate of the Mishnah (hence of the Tosefta or Talmud) dealing with a specific subject and subdivided into chapters.

MESSIAH—The eschatological king who is to rule over Israel at the end of days. The messianic king would destroy the enemies of Israel and establish a paradise-like reign of peace and prosperity.

MIKVEH—A pool of running water containing natural (not pumped) water—that is, spring water—serving for immersion for the purpose of purification. Today it serves mainly women who come to purify themselves from their monthly menstruation.

MISHNAH—Not so much a code as a textbook, giving the essence of the Oral Law as it was known to the sages of the time. It recorded conflicting opinions and very often named the disputants. Compiled by Judah Ha-Nasi (The President) by the year 220 CE.

OLAM HABA (THE WORLD TO COME)—The concept of *Olam Haba* is different from that of Heaven or Paradise, which is the abode of departed souls pending the advent of the "coming age." The *Olam Haba* designates the spiritual world to which the soul arrives after death. The belief in the *Olam Haba* is one of the principles of Judaism. In the *Olam Haba* the pious will be rewarded for their good deeds and the wicked will be punished.

The *Olam Hazeh* (the current empirical world) is a corridor leading to the *Olam Haba*. The Gemara says that in the *Olam Haba* there is no food and no drink, no hatred, and no envy, no negotiations and no reproduction, only *Tzaddikim* (righteous ones) sitting with diadems on their heads enjoying the beauty of the Divine Presence.

ORTHODOXY—Modern designation for the strictly traditional branch of Jewry united in their acceptance of the Divine Law in its written and oral forms, as immutable and binding for all times.

PASSOVER (PESACH)—First of the three Pilgrim Festivals (on the 14th of Nissan), commemorating the Exodus of the Children of Israel from Egypt, observed for eight days in the Diaspora and seven days in Israel and by Reform Jews. The *seder* ceremony celebrated on the first night(s) of the festival is the most important home ceremony in the liturgical year. Special dietary laws apply to the entire duration of the festival. They are (a) the strict prohibition against eating (or keeping at home) any leaven; and (b) the commandment to eat *matzah* for the duration of the festival. The first and the last day of Pesach are considered holy days and all work is prohibited.

RABBI AKIVA (4 CE–135 CE)—A *tanna*. Laid the foundations for the exposition of the Oral Law as later codified in the Mishnah and is credited with having arranged the Oral Law into its divisions of Mishnah, Tosefta, Sifra, and Sifrey. He is especially noted for his hermeneutic exposition of Scripture, finding a basis for the Oral Law in almost every peculiarity or superfluity in the language of the Bible. His method was opposed by his great contemporary Rabbi Ishmael, who taught that "Scripture spoke in the language of men"—that is, it must be interpreted straightforwardly and literally. He was a prime supporter of the Bar Kokhba revolt, arrested as a rebel and tortured by the Romans, imprisoned for a very long period, and finally executed in Caesarea. His martyrdom became a lasting legend of exemplary love of God and faithfulness to Judaism.

RABBI KOOK, AVRAHAM YITZHAK (1865–1935)—Chief Rabbi of Palestine (from 1921) and a spiritual leader whose personality, thought, and writings appealed to religious and nonreligious alike. He called for a Judaism to include all the variegated expressions of the Jewish religious genius— its law, legends, poetry, mysticism, etc. Kook was inclined to see the hidden mystical streams of Jewish thought as the "soul" of Judaism, as part of the "fuller and deeper" Torah.

RABBI NACHMAN OF BRATZLAV (1772–1810)—A great-great-grandson of the Baal Shem Tov, he was one of the most original of the Hasidic leaders. He regarded himself as the only true interpreter of his teachings, thus incurring the hostility of other Hasidic rabbis by his criticism of them. He stressed simple faith and prayer as opposed to intellectualism and developed the theory of the *Tzaddik* as the intermediary between man and God. His outstanding contribution to Hasidic literature is his collection of folk tales (*Sippurei Ma'asiyot*)—homely parables which his followers believe enshrine the most recondite and esoteric mysteries.

RABBI SIMEON BAR YOHAI (2ND CENTURY CE)—*Tanna*, pupil of Rabbi Akiva. Lived and conducted his school at Tekoa in Upper Galilee. The *halakhic* Midrashim, Sifrey, and Mekhilta evolved from the teachings of his yeshiva, which was noted for systematic classification of *halakhot* and attempts to adduce a rational basis for the Torah. Bar Yohai had a reputation as a miracle worker. For speaking against the Romans, he was condemned to death, and he and his son, Elazar, consequently went into hiding. They spent twelve to thirteen years in a cave in Peki'in until the death decree was annulled. Many legends were woven around this period. Kabbalists attribute the origin of the *Book of Zohar* to this period. His traditional death date on Lag Ba'Omer is a traditional folk celebration in Miron, in the Galilee, highlighted with bonfires.

RASHI (ABBREV. FOR RABBI SHLOMO YITZHAKI—1040–1104)—A French biblical and Talmudic scholar. He founded his own yeshiva, which attracted many students in his native town of Troyes. He is famous for his interpretative works. His commentaries excel all others by the lucidity and precision with which they explain even the most intricate subject. In some cases he even included interpretations from the Midrash. His commentary on the Bible was the first dated Hebrew book printed (1475) and it was translated into Latin. It was said of Rashi that but for his commentary, the Talmud would have been forgotten.

REBBE (THE YIDDISH WORD FOR RABBI)—Term used for Hasidic leaders and spiritual guides. The *rebbe* or *tzaddik* is not necessarily a *halakhic* scholar or teacher, but guides his followers by virtue of the spiritual power and holiness thought to be inherent in him.

THE REBBE OF LUBAVICH—Lubavich is a Russian village near Mogilev, which was, until the Soviet Revolution, the seat of the Schneersohn dynasty, leaders of the Habad Hasidim. The Rabbi of Lubavich has settled since in New York and functions as a spiritual guide and teacher. The spiritual life of the Lubavichers centers on the study of the founder's writings (*Tanya*). This is one of the most active Hasidic groups, maintaining schools, yeshivas, and orphanages.

REFORM JUDAISM—Religious trend advocating modification of Orthodox tradition in conformity with the exigencies of contemporary life and thought. The essential difference between Reform and Orthodox Judaism revolves around the authority of the *halakhah*; Orthodoxy maintains the Divine authority of the *halakhah* in both its biblical and rabbinic expressions, Reform Judaism subjects religious law and customs to the judgment of man. It attempts to differentiate between those elements of the law that are "eternal" and those legal forms and customs that it believes are the product of a particular age.

SEPHARDI—The Jews of the Iberian peninsula and their descendants came to be known as Sephardi in distinction to the Jews of the Franco-German tradition, who are known as Ashkenazi. The Sephardi Jewry represents a continuation of the Babylonian tradition. After the expulsion of the Jews from Spain in 1492, the word *Sephardi* was given wider connotation as the Jews from Spain imposed their culture and traditions upon the Jewish communities of North Africa and the Middle East. The word *Sephardi* today is thus frequently used for a Jew belonging to one of the Oriental communities which adopted the Sephardi rite, whether or not the community is originally of Spanish provenance.

SIDDUR—The Hebrew prayerbook; it contains the entire liturgy used in the synagogue and at home, including many nonobligatory prayers.

TANNAIM—*Tanna* (Aramaic: "one who studies and teaches," especially the Oral Law) refers to sages whose views are compiled in the Mishnah and *baraita*. The period of the *Tannaim* began after Hillel and Shammai and ended with the generation after Rabbi Judah Ha-Nasi, in the second century.

THE TEMPLE—The House of the Lord, the sanctuary on Mount Moriah in Jerusalem, was built by King Solomon in the tenth century BCE and was the center of the nation's spiritual and religious life. The ritual there included sacrifices. It was destroyed by the Babylonians in 587 BCE. The Shivat Zion people who returned from Babylonia rebuilt it in about 515 BCE, but it was destroyed by Titus, the Roman Emperor, on the 9th of the month of Av in 70 CE. The day of the destruction has ever since been a day of fasting and prayer. The Temple area is now the site of the Mosque of Omar, erected c. 700 CE.

TORAH—Hebrew word referring to the Bible. Its literal meaning is "teaching," "instruction," or "guidance." In rabbinic literature Torah is used in a variety of senses, all based on the general understanding of Torah as the guidance and teaching imparted to Israel by Divine Revelation. It designates the Pentateuch as distinct from the other two main sections of the Hebrew Bible—the Prophets and the Writings (Hagiographa).

TOSAFOT [HEB.: "ADDITIONS"]—Beginning as additional interpretations and complements to Rashi's *Commentary on the Talmud,* it grew into a much wider work, much more than just an interpretation. The Tosafot were the combined work of French and German Jewish scholars in the twelfth and thirteenth centuries, the first of whom were descendants of Rashi, starting with his grandchildren. The Tosafot are printed on the outer side of the Talmud page while on the inner side there appears the Rashi commentary.

WARSAW GHETTO—The Jewish ghetto, a special urban quarter for the sole residence of Jews. During World War II the Nazis erected new ghettos in Polish and west Russian towns which served as prisons until the inhabitants' transfer to the death camps. The Warsaw Ghetto was famous for its rebellion, headed by Mordekhai Anilevich, against the Nazis; the rebellion was suppressed and all its participants were put to death.

YESHIVA—The oldest institution for higher learning of the Written and Oral Jewish Law.

YOM KIPPUR—Day of Atonement. The most solemn occasion of the Jewish calendar—the 10th of the month of Tishri. The main features of the day are the "five mortifications:" abstention from food, drink, marital intercourse, anointing with oil, and wearing leather shoes. During the 25-hour fast, five services of prayer take place; the first of these, in the Evening Service, is preceded by the recitation of *Kol Nidrei*. The prayers of the day stress confession of sins and supplications for forgiveness on behalf of the whole congregation of Israel.

ZIONIST MOVEMENT—Movement to secure the return of the Jews to the Land of Israel. Modern political Zionism was founded by Theodor Herzl at the First Zionist Congress (1897), aimed at a peaceful political solution of the "Jewish Problem."

ZOHAR, THE BOOK OF—A Kabbalistic work composed of several literary units recognized by Kabbalists as the most important of mystical teaching. It contains exchanges and reflections by a group of second-century rabbis and scholars led by Simeon bar Yohai, exposing the esoteric meaning of Scripture. Modern research dates the book to the thirteenth century.

y

INDEX